COPING WITH THE INTERVIEW

COPING WITH
THE INTERVIEW

JOHN KEEFE

THE ROSEN PUBLISHING GROUP, Inc.
New York

Published in 1971, 1979, 1982 by The Rosen Publishing Group, Inc.
29 East 21st Street, New York, N.Y. 10010

Revised Edition 1982

Library of Congress Cataloging in Publication Data

Keefe, John E
    Coping with the interview.

    Edition for 1971 published under title: The teenager and the interview.
    Bibliography: p.
    SUMMARY: Advice for teenagers on filling out job applications, making resumes, responding to interviews, and other aspects of finding employment.
    1. Vocational guidance—Juvenile literature.
2. Applications for positions—Juvenile literature.
[1. Vocational guidance. 2. Applications for positions] I. Title.

HF5381.2.K43   1979   650'.14'024055   78–14297
ISBN 0–8239–0475–X

Dedicated to Counselors
with the hope that they use with
caution the power entrusted to them—
guiding the Teenager

Preface to Revised Edition

Since this book was originally published in 1971, many technological
and demographic changes have taken place. We have made the necessary changes in pertinent facts and figures and revised the statistics
and salary ranges upward or downward depending on current conditions. The figures used are the most recent available.

Note: This book was
originally published as
*The Teenager and the
Interview*. The
title change reflects
the updating of the
content and its thrust.

About the Author

By virtue of his training and his teaching and industrial experience, John Keefe possesses an excellent background for writing a book designed as a vocational guide for teenagers seeking guidance in job hunting.

After receiving a B.A. in Education at Muhlenberg College, he earned a Master's Degree in Vocational Guidance at Temple University, at the same time teaching Romance Languages at Haverford High School in Pennsylvania, as well as coaching football and track.

Finding the classroom confining, he applied his graduate work to the private sector and began work in 1951 as a Personnel Interviewer for the Radio Corporation of America. He progressed to the positions of Employment Manager, Wage and Salary Manager, Personnel Manager, and to the position of Manager, National Employment, with the RCA Service Company, a Division of RCA. With the dynamic surge in educational areas and the urgent need for trained personnel men, he reentered the educational field and is presently Coordinator of Work-Study Programs in the Haverford Township School District, Havertown, Pennsylvania.

He is a frequent speaker at career and guidance forums and acts as a consultant and lecturer on vocational curriculum and in the specialized area of personnel practices in public education. He is the author of two books in the Richards Rosen *Aim High* Series: *Aim for a Job as an Electronic Technician* and *Aim for a Job in Appliance Service.* His most recent book published by Richards Rosen Press is *The Joy of Work,* written with Stanley J. Stein. In addition, he has published articles in various management and educational professional journals.

He is a member of many educational and management associations.

Contents

COPING WITH THE INTERVIEW

CHAPTER I

How to Look for—and Find—That Job

Applying for and getting the job you want is no easy task. You can minimize your searching if you plan your approach carefully. There are "tricks of the trade," which, used properly, can save you much time and energy.

In the chapters following are helpful hints on the techniques of getting a specific type of job. This chapter contains information that is more general and will give you an overall approach to your task of findng a job.

Employment service is the process of getting together the people who want jobs and the employers who need people to perform jobs. The employer is looking for qualified persons to interview; if you know what type of job he is trying to fill and what kind of person he is seeking, then you hold the key to employment.

You must be resourceful in your approach and utilize many methods in order to hit on the job you want. For example, since American industry is cost-conscious and governed by the profit-and-loss philosophy, the employer will seek low-cost sources of procurement. Most job hunters are inclined to look first in the "Want Ads" section of the newspaper. An employer uses this source as a last resort because it costs money.

Let us look at the various sources.

LOW-COST SOURCES FOR FINDING NEW EMPLOYEES

Schools

An employer who utilizes teenage employees will normally turn to schools as a prime source of workers. He tries to match his period of greatest need to the time when the largest number of persons will be available—June or July. So it is wise for you to begin your hunt in March or April for June openings. Many employers will recruit at the school offices or will supply counselors or principals with a list of vacancies. Check the school bulletin board regularly to look for possibilities.

Employment Agencies: Public and Private

Since you will be new at job hunting, you may not know of the services offered by the United States Employment Service (USES). We speak so often of the employment office in connection with unemployment compensation that we forget that the USES is highly geared toward job placement. It is cost-free and not only has information on jobs being filled locally, but employment information on a nationwide basis as well. Another service the USES offers is information regarding Civil Service opportunities. The USES and affiliated State Employment Services have a network of approximately 2,000 employment offices throughout the country, with centers in every state.

Besides job placement, the USES has an extensive job-counseling service. The General Aptitude Test Battery (GATB) is used to determine job aptitude, skills, and areas of interest. The GATB is described in greater detail in Chapter IV.

In many cities certain private organizations help teenagers with jobs. They can help because they represent a natural gathering of business people or community leaders who may be attuned to job possibilities—Rotary, Lions Club, Kiwanis, Chamber of Commerce, YMCA, YWCA, YMHA, YWHA, Salvation Army, church groups, PTA's, and veterans' organizations.

You can seek out those organizations and let them know you are available and the type of job you are looking for.

Groups that specialize in seeking out job possibilities for minority groups are in most cases interracial and will give service to any job seeker regardless of race.

The National Urban League, Inc. has more than sixty chapters throughout the United States and has a history of job placements from the lowest skills to top-level scientists. The National Association for the Advancement of Colored People (NAACP) offers the same service. Similar groups include the Equal Opportunity Merit Employment Committees found in major cities.

Several community groups have taken the initiative in providing job training for minority and underskilled people. Particularly outstanding is the work of the Reverend Leon H. Sullivan, a Baptist minister, who founded the Opportunities Industrialization Center (OIC) in Philadelphia, Pennsylvania.

The Center, which opened in 1964, trains thousands each year in such practical fields as drafting, electronics, machine shop, and teletype operations. The Center's staff is composed of competent counselors, instructors, and job-placement officers who are in contact

COURTESY U.S. NAVY

The guidance counselor is the focal point in providing information to teenagers.

with employers in order to determine the types of training needed and where OIC graduates can be placed.

In Boston, Massachusetts, a private organization called Jobs Clearing House, Inc. is dedicated to matching workers to jobs. In its first year of operation, it found jobs for six hundred of its seventeen hundred registrants; 98 percent of those placed were Negroes. The categories of jobs ranged from production workers to retail sales people to management trainees.

In discussing the minority citizen, other groups besides the Negro are to be considered. Identifiable minority groups in the United States are Orientals, American Indians, and Spanish-Americans.

The Bureau of Indian Affairs has programs to train American Indians and Eskimos in skilled occupations.

The Spanish-speaking groups are most prevalent in the Southwest and the New York City area. Texas, with Negroes and Latin Americans accounting for more than two million of its population, is making great use of its minority citizens. State representatives work in conjunction with organizations such as the GI Forum, Politi-

COURTESY CREATIVE PLAYTHINGS, INC.
PRINCETON, NEW JERSEY

A teenager performs drafting duties as part of a high-school work/study co-operative program.

cal Association of Spanish Speaking Organizations, American Friends, The League of United Latin American Citizens, and others.

Private Employment Agencies

Private employment agencies are those agencies that charge a fee for their services. They charge money because they effect the bringing together of the applicant and the employer. They know of job markets and can be helpful in pinpointing a specific work locality, type of work, and so on. Many are affiliated with national organizations and can satisfy geographical preferences if you have any.

Placement fees are required only if actual emplyoment is obtained. The fees vary throughout the country and are regulated by various state laws. The amount of the fee further depends upon the starting salary. For example, a job paying a yearly salary of $7,000 will have a placement fee ranging from 5 percent to 10 percent of the first year's salary.

If you should register with a private agency and be proposed for a specific job, determine whether you or the prospective employer will pay the fee. Some employers will pay the whole amount, part of it, or none of it, depending upon the supply and demand of the particular applicant being sought.

In return for the placement fee, private agencies can minimize your job searching and save you much time. Lists of private employment agencies can be found in the Sunday editions of newspapers or in the Yellow Pages of the telephone directory.

Personal Contacts

There is an old saying: "What are friends for?" Well, they may be helpful in supplying you with job information. Friends and neighbors who work in particular firms should be contacted and made aware that you are job hunting. Many times—especially in a tight labor market—employees are encouraged to seek out applicants.

These formalized personnel programs are called Internal Referral Programs. On occasion the employee making a referral who is ultimately hired receives an award of some kind—a savings bond, a cash award, an extra day of vacation. In the case of scarce specialists such as computer personnel, engineers, and scientists, valuable awards such as a color TV set or even an expense-paid trip to Bermuda are sometimes given.

Check such people as postmen or milkmen, policemen or taxi drivers. They come in contact with a lot of people and may be able to give you leads.

Remember, those people will only tell you which door to knock on. It is up to you to get the job.

Personal Job Hunting

This approach is one of the most difficult. It may be compared with "door-to-door" selling or "beating the bushes." It can be frustrating. But you may also be lucky. You must zero in on what you want.

Probably the most commonly used approach for job hunting is the "casual" or "walk-in" method. This is direct application to an employer by appearing at his place of business. It is strictly a hit-or-miss proposition unless you know that the firm is seeking a particular type of help. If you use this approach, go prepared with some in-

Food services provide interesting positions on permanent, temporary, or part-time basis.

formation about the firm: what it manufactures and the type of skill required.

The Yellow Pages, Chamber of Commerce booklets, industry directories, union lists, and similar listings will help you to find what you are looking for. Do not go only to large firms. Check the small ones as well. Job seekers have a tendency to gravitate to large firms, and, as a result, large firms often have a backlog of applications from which they can draw. Competition is less in a smaller firm.

Direct mail solicitation is another method. Check Chapter II on applications and résumés for hints to help you with this approach.

With the advent of the shopping-center complex, the supermarket bulletin board has become an institution. Here you can place an ad —usually a 3 x 5 card—and look over the others that are posted.

Sometimes wondrous things are to be found there. Also keep an eye open for help-wanted signs in store windows.

Another technique is to have cards printed publicizing the services you have to offer. You may place them in mail boxes or on car windows in parking lots, at sports events, shopping centers, etc.

Newspapers periodically run a special campaign for teenagers whereby they will allow you to run an ad of one or two lines free of charge. This is common in many communities during the spring so that teenagers may have a good opportunity to advertise for summer jobs.

If your local newspaper does not provide this service (you might make the suggestion to an enterprising ad manager if they don't), you can place your own in a newspaper using the "Situations Wanted" section. This is not normally a highly productive source, but is the "rifle" approach to job hunting—and who knows? the right person might read your ad. You can get in touch with your local newspaper to find out the rates charged for ads.

Employer-Cost Sources of Procurement

In order to solicit applicants, the employer must pay in some way or other.

Help Wanted Ads

This is another of the most common ways to look for a job. The fact that the employer is paying for an ad means that he has used up his supply of applications. The ad might ask you to apply in person (if he needs applicants as quickly as possible) or to write or call for an appointment.

The prospective employer might place a "blind ad," which does not identify the firm. This may mean that he wants to screen applicants "quietly" and thus not be obligated to answer all the applicants. It may also mean that he wants to keep his present employees from learning of the opening.

The newspaper is the quickest way to find job openings. However, you must review the whole section, since jobs will be listed under various sections. For example, an employer seeking someone in "Appliance Service" might place listings under the following headings—yet need a person with the same qualifications for all:

Serviceman	Air-Conditioning Mechanic
Appliance Repairman	Refrigerator Technician
Appliance Technician	Oil Burner Technician
Mechanic	

Using the job of Secretary as another example, you might find the following headings:

Secretary	Administrative Assistant
Stenographer	Steno-Clerk
Gal Friday	

Most ads for skilled and unskilled workers will be in the classified (Help Wanted) section of the newspaper. Professional or highly skilled administrative and managerial positions often appear in a display ad on the sports page or financial page, with a small cross-reference ad in the classified section. However, ads of this type will seldom or never offer jobs that would be of interest to a teenager.

People advertise most intensively in Sunday papers. That is the best place to look. Go over the paper thoroughly. When reading the want ads, you must not miss a line or you may miss a job.

Do not count on just one newspaper. Even though a specific paper may have good circulation, it may not be the best one for want ads. When job hunting, buy all the papers published in your town or city and hunt from there.

Trade journals carry job listings to cover special occupations dealing with a particular trade or profession. There are hundreds of such publications. Training opportunities for teenagers are often found listed there.

This book is designed to give you a wide approach to job seeking. Other methods exist, to be sure, but the message here is to encourage you to be resourceful and make your own way. It is up to you.

CHAPTER II

The Employment Application and the Résumé

Completing the employment application is not always as easy as it sounds. Developing an effective résumé requires a bit of organization plus some concentration. This chapter will concern itself with a close look at the employment application and résumé. We shall make a detailed analysis of what lies behind the questions to be answered on the application and give you many ideas and hints as to the most effective way to prepare your résumé.

The employment application is really a test in itself—especially if it is to be sent by mail rather than presented in person. You must sell yourself through this piece of paper if you are to get an interview. *Remember that the interview is your first goal.* Getting the job is the last step.

Even though a personnel interviewer is trained not to prejudge or to rely on first impressions, the temptation is great to do so when he is confronted with an application that is incomplete, soiled, misspelled, or torn.

Keep in mind the neatness of the form. Type it if possible—or print it. Avoid erasures. If you must erase, use the proper eraser for the type of paper you are using. Read the questions carefully before answering them. It is a good idea to write your answers on a separate piece of paper before filling in the printed form.

What Is Expected?

Name—You certainly do not need help on this—although it can sometimes be a problem to an employer. For example, a job applicant might have had a change of name by legal action or through marriage. A woman who had worked under her maiden name for an employer may find that he denies that anyone with her new name ever worked for him.

Address—You can expect a request for one or two addresses—a permanent or a temporary address. This can present a problem in the case of students who are living away at school and planning to work away from home at a summer job. In any event, give an address at which you can be reached at any time or from which you know your mail will be forwarded. Also, be sure to list postal zip codes—they seem to be here to stay.

COURTESY KELLY SERVICES

Kelly Services offer everything in marketing support from product demonstrations to survey taking.

Telephone—In the interest of time, the personnel manager will frequently contact applicants by phone. It is very important that you list a number at which you always can be reached, directly or indirectly. Give the best calling hours if you are away from the listed number for extended periods. Also, make sure that a responsible person answers the phone and relays the messages. From the author's experience, many jobs have been lost when the person was never notified of the call.

Social Security Number—The first thing you should do after being assigned your Social Security number is to memorize it. It should be printed indelibly in your mind. This has become just as important as—and in some cases more important than—your name. Since most information is computerized today, far less chance of duplication is involved if the Social Security number is used. Duplicate names are common and can present problems: Look at the telephone directory of any large town or city and see the numbers of Smiths, Cohens, and Browns.

Further, unless you are paid in cash, you will probably never receive a paycheck without a Social Security number on it. Obtaining a Social Security number is easy, and age is not a factor. It would be well to apply for a number as soon as you can secure the proper form at the post office. Without a Social Security number, your chances of getting a job will be slim.

Marital Status—This question may not be important to most teenagers, but there are valid reasons for asking it. Two incomes may be needed to keep up with today's high cost of living—especially for young married couples. Most widows and divorcees are good employment risks—particularly if they have a family to support.

Type of Work Desired—This is very important. Do not undersell your talents and do not be afraid to extend yourself. Be more specific than to apply for "general work" or "anything." Analyze what you can do—drive a vehicle, assemble parts, do manual labor, be a trades helper, typist, secretary, laboratory aide, auto mechanic, farmhand, printer.

Set your sights high—but be prepared to take a lesser job.

Find out ahead of time what openings exist and apply for those vacancies if you think you have any chance of qualifying.

Number of Dependents and Ages of Dependents or Children—This can be a plus or a minus. Most of those reading this book will be responsible for just themselves. However, when an employer is considering a woman who has children to support, her responsibility can be a plus, for she will make a great effort to be at work regularly. On the other hand, it can be a minus if there are babysitting problems or children must be got off to school. It is not a matter of discrimination but sound business practice. Let's face it.

Driver's License—If you are of age, the ability to drive can be a deciding factor in being chosen for the job. For instance, a person who cannot drive a vehicle with a manual gearshift may limit his job possibilities.

Condition of Health—If you are in normal health and seldom suffer illness, list "excellent" or "very good" under this section. The person who lists "good" may give the impression that he is prone to less than "good" health. Many applications ask for the "number of days of work missed during the last two years." The reason for this question is obvious.

You may be asked whether you have had any surgical operations or diseases. These could be contributing factors in deciding whether to employ you in a specific job. If you have an allergy, for instance, or cannot lift heavy objects, you would not be suitable for certain types of work.

Wearing eyeglasses can be a factor in deciding employment. The job may require safety glasses, or it may bar a person who wears glasses because the work atmosphere is steamy.

A physical examination is a matter of course in most firms. This test can range from a routine general checkup to the other extreme of a technical eye examination testing not only visual acuity and depth perception but also such other conditions as color blindess.

Height—Weight—This is another blank on the application that may seem routine. The information is very necessary, however, because you might be too short, too tall, too light, or too heavy for a specific job. For example, a small-parts assembler is usually a person of small stature who has slender hands indicating the finger dexterity necessary to do delicate work. A job that must be performed in a confined area requires a person of a particular height. A fat person cannot handle a job in a situation where he does not have enough room to operate. A job that requires lifting needs a person with special physical qualifications. The driver of a large vehicle must be a long-legged person. And so it goes.

Date of Birth—In most states, it is illegal to ask the date of birth because of possible discrimination against the worker. When age is a bona fide occupational qualification, however, the question may be posed. This is usually the case with teenagers because of child-labor laws and other age regulations. Check Chapter V, which deals with summer and part-time jobs.

Later in the chapter we shall discuss the various discrimination laws, in order to give you an idea of the reasons behind those regulations.

Arrests—The need for this information is obvious. In addition to the moral issues involved, the job in question may be one that requires a security clearance. A previous arrest or arrests can prevent the issuance of such a clearance. The employer is not interested in such violations as illegal parking but, rather, more serious offenses. Do not omit any arrests—and especially do not omit any convictions. If you do omit such information, it will catch up with you through reference checks and will result in your being fired for misrepresentation or falsification of information. The same guidelines apply to service veterans and the court-martial as to the civilian and arrests. Further, some firms may require a polygraph (lie detector test) where theft may occur, drugs are manufactured, and so forth.

Friends or Relatives Employed by the Firm—This can be a negative as well as a positive factor. Be sure that the person or persons you list are reliable workers. Be certain also that the people you list are aware that their names are being used. If you are unable to reach such a person by phone, write him a note telling him what you have done. If you know in advance that you may want to use someone's name as reference, get permission to do so.

On the positive side, employers regard internal referrals as one of the best sources of manpower procurement. The fact that you list the name of a valued employee—and that he will endorse you —will be an asset in getting a job.

Previous Employment at This Firm—This is important to the interviewer, especially in a large firm. Your previous work record with the firm may open or close the door for you on your return to the organization. Be sure to answer the question truthfully. If you have had previous employment and do not say so, your "slip of the pencil" will be discovered when records are checked.

Salary Expected—In counseling young people as well as experienced workers, this is the question I am asked most ofen.

How *do* you answer the question? It depends. The experienced worker usually knows the "market price" for his services. However, the difficult point is whether to oversell or undersell himself on salary.

If possible, he should find out in advance what the salary structure is at the firm. A newspaper ad or an employment counselor should be of help in this regard.

Since most teenagers have little to offer in the way of experience, they are usually paid the prevailing wage. This should be your answer, then—"the prevailing wage." Usually there is a set rate of pay—the firm's established rate, or the legal minimum wage for the type of work performed.

If a firm has a good wage and salary program, it will pay the area's "going rate" for various occupations. The firm that attempts to hire employees at a "cheap price" will have a high turnover rate and spend much time looking for new help.

*Shift Desired—Hours Available for Work—*You may not get a choice of work hours in your first several jobs. Large multishift firms have a "shift-preference" system, and most new employees must accept jobs on the second or third shifts. Since these are the least desirable shifts, however, they usually command premium pay for the hardship endured. (See Chapter X.)

Summer and part-time jobs on the second shift (usually 3 or 3:30 P.M. to 11 P.M. or midnight) or third shift (usually from 11 P.M. or midnight to 7 or 7:30 A.M.) can be the most desirable work hours for teenagers, since you have the daylight hours to yourself. The premium pay can also be a greater factor, since you want to save as much money as possible in a short time.

You must be certain, however, to get proper rest and nutrition when working the odd shifts. It is easy to become rundown under such conditions.

Study the eating and sleeping habits of professional athletes (basketball, baseball, and hockey players), who are really "night people." It is most interesting to learn how they keep in top physical condition despite odd work hours—changes in time zones, sleeping under varying conditions every few nights, eating in a variety of restaurants, and the like.

Another question usually asked in conjunction with this one is whether your spouse (if you have one) works and on what shift. Why? If you are both working and are on different shifts, it could work out that you would see each other only once in seven days or on weekends. One of you would probably be sleeping when the other comes home. This type of employment arrangement does not last long, for anyone quickly tires of a home life reduced to the absolute minimum.

How Will You Travel to Work? This question is aimed at several possibilities:

(1) Public transportation to the job may not be available, and you may have to rely on someone else if you do not own a car. In such a case your reliability depends upon the person with whom you are able to get a ride. If he has a good attendance record, so will you.

(2) You may have a revoked driver's license, which could make your situation even worse.

(3) If you live at a considerable distance and/or work an odd shift, special travel arrangements may have to be made if you do not have your own car. Public transportation schedules may not dovetail with your work schedules.

In Case of Emergency Notify—Hopefully this information may never be used in your case. List a responsible person who can be relied upon in the event of an emergency. Give alternatives if you have any doubt as to availability or reliability. Also be prepared to list phone numbers, since the person may have to be reached within a short time.

Date Available for Work—A matter of ethics is involved in answering this question if you are already employed. Proper notice must be given to your present employer. In most full-time jobs, two weeks' notice is the normal practice unless your employer already has someone to take your place or can find someone in a shorter period of time.

Do not leave a job without giving notice. It might hurt your future references, and it would jeopardize your chances if you should ever want to be employed by the organization again.

Of course, for a summer or seasonal job, you would probably be immediately available, since you are anxious to earn money as quickly as possible.

Education Section—You should be prepared to list all of your education—formal or otherwise—from grade school to the present. Be sure to emphasize any special courses you may have taken—a summer typing course, a Red Cross safety program, mechanical drawing, etc. Further, know your class standing or final academic average if you are a high-school, secretarial-school, or technical-school graduate. Be prepared to give an accounting of your current grades if you have not yet graduated.

If asked, specify your best grades—mathematics, mechanical drawing, typing, English, or whatever. There may be some significance here that could help you land a special job.

Work Experience—Here you must list all possibilities that might lead to a job. Do not underestimate your experience in part-time jobs. Work that you may have done around your home or helped a neighbor with—painting, gardening, building a patio, planting shrubs, typing, dress designing, sewing, cooking, baby sitting—can

Efficiency-guaranteed services of every description are provided throughout the United States and Canada by the Kelly Girls.

count for job experience. Just because you may not have been paid does not mean that you did not learn. The fact that you have not worked at a full-time job does not mean that you are inexperienced.

I have in mind a young man who approached me about job counseling. He was 14, mature for his age, and tired of staying home with his mother and the television set. He felt somewhat inferior about his qualifications for a camp counseling job until he assessed his background. When he began to analyze all the things he had been doing for most of those 14 years, he found he was able to complete many items on the employment form and, to his great satisfaction, got a job as a junior counselor.

When he analyzed them, these were his qualifications:

(1) He had a musical background—he had studied the accordion for three years.
(2) He had been a Boy Scout and was familiar with camping, some arts and crafts, hiking, and games.
(3) In junior high school he had gone out for football and track and was familiar with several other sports through indirect exposure.
(4) He was mechanically inclined and had completed several successful science projects both in and out of school.
(5) He was large for his age and was capable of performing heavy manual labor. He had been taught how to use a shovel, pick, wheelbarrow, and ax by his father.

After he had completed the application, he was surprised to find how much he had to offer.

School Activities and Honors—These factors weigh heavily for a teenager during any type of interview, because he must substitute something for actual work experience. In addition to what has been mentioned above about sports, music, and other interests, good grades show a sense of responsibility and achievement. Honors or special courses (typing, mechanical drawing, machine repair) can contribute toward presenting a better picture of yourself.

Be sure to mention any special honors you may have had—homeroom president, honor roll, sport captain, student committees. List such activities as chorus, glee club, library club, radio club, automobile club. The interviewer himself may have a special interest in one of these areas, and you may be able to capitalize on it. If you were in a Work-Study program, this will carry weight.

Hobbies—Interests—These tie in with school activities and honors. They can show responsibility, interest, and initiative, depending upon the complexity of the special interest or hobby. A liking for tinkering or working with autos or clocks can help in jobs that require mechanical aptitude. Photography is another special interest that may help. If you do your own developing, be sure to say so. Any special skills or licenses, such as an ability to operate office machines or tools, should be listed.

If you design or make your own clothes, or cook and bake, these can be translated into job possibilities. An interest in gardening can lead toward a greenhouse job, farm work, or a job as a groundsman. A strong interest in science may help in acquiring a place in a hospital or laboratory.

Military Experience—Military experience is viewed positively. Persons who have undergone this experience have acquired a maturity that is difficult to find. Also, you may have had some special training—electronics, auto mechanics, drafting, typing, or other.

References—These are extremely important, especially if you have never been employed before. Most interviewers rely heavily upon past employers for reference information and place less faith in personal references. The reason for this is that applicants naturally list persons who will give good recommendations as personal reference. Again, be sure to obtain prior permission.

At any rate, choose carefully the names you list and—above all —*obtain permission from the person before using his name.* As mentioned earlier in the chapter, if you are taken unaware and have to use a name without first asking permission, get in touch with the person immediately to tell him that you have done so. Not obtaining permission is a strong breach of etiquette and might cost you the job. It reveals that you lack the common courtesies or social skills.

Be prepared to list the address, occupation, and phone number of the person used as reference.

Written Evaluation—Some employment applications will have a section asking you to give a short handwritten self-evaluation or biographical sketch.

Prepare a draft of what you want to express. Get all your thoughts down and organize them so you can place your finished work on the application in a neat fashion—without erasures or grammatical errors and with the proper spacing.

The employer will be looking for such points as your handwriting, grammar, and the ability to express yourself in one hundred to two hundred words.

Willingness to Travel—In the early stages of your work career, there will be little likelihood of your traveling any great distances. However, expect the question. There might also be a question as to what percent of the time you are willing to travel.

Foreign Language Proficiency—Read, write, speak, foreign languages? Every little bit helps, and you never know when this ability could be the deciding factor in getting a job over someone else with equal qualifications except for the language skill.

Special Skills—Ham radio operator, typing proficiency, shorthand, Speedwriting, ability to operate office machines, special licenses

COURTESY NEW JERSEY BELL TELEPHONE COMPANY

A student operator is given an assist from a service assistant in placing a long-distance phone call.

that you may hold, certificates of special ability—any of these should be listed.

Our local paper recently carried the story of two 14-year-old boys who had passed the exams to be ham operators. Frequently, you read of teenage boys and girls who earn their pilot's licenses. Having the ability to direct a project for a Junior Achievement Chapter would indeed be a special skill. The number of skills virtually equals the number of teenagers applying for jobs. Just stop to think what you can do that is special.

PREVIOUS EMPLOYMENT INFORMATION

This is being treated as a special section because of its importance.
Previous Occupations—Know the exact titles and full names of
your previous supervisors. If you were a clerk typist, list this and not
simply "clerk." The same is true of any technical work. For example,
do not list simply "technician," but "electronic technician" or "X-ray
technician."

Be sure to account for all periods of employment. No time gaps
should occur unless you were actually unemployed. If there are gaps,
be prepared to account for them.

Description of Duties—Again, be specific and do not generalize.
Do not sell yourself short. If you were an assembler and did a lot of
testing and measuring, mention this. Give the details of your job.
You can elaborate without generalizing.

Reasons for Leaving—This is one of the most carefully scruti-
nized portions of the application. It tells many things:

(1) Are you a "job-hopper"?
(2) Are you a "griper"?
(3) Can you stick to one job?
(4) Do you avoid responsibility?
(5) Can you get along with people and work within a group
effort?

You should be truthful as to why you left previous employers,
since reference checks will reveal the reason for your leaving in case
you have not.

For those of you who are just beginning your work careers, here
are words that are "red flags" to employers: You left because of:

Dissatisfaction
Personal reasons
Too much resopnsibility for amount of pay
Work was too hard
Personality conflict
Poor working conditions
Not enough pay (yet you may now be prepared to take another
job at the same or lower rate of pay!).

Closing Statement—Most employment applications have a closing statement to the effect that, if you have given any false answers or statements, these misrepresentations can be cause for termination. Do not hide anything. Misleading information is usually uncovered during reference checks.

You can also expect a statement in this section that gives the employer the permission to get in touch with your past employers—except perhaps your present employer. Read this portion carefully because, if you are seeking work elsewhere, you will in all likelihood not want your present employer to have knowledge of this until you give notice of termination.

Signature and Date—Do not forget to sign and date the application. Sounds simple, but experience has shown that two or three out of every ten applicants neglect to complete this final portion of the form.

Legal Aspects of the Employment Application—Many states have laws that forbid asking employment information dealing with sex, age, race, color, creed, or national origin. The laws were instituted because of discriminating hiring practices of some employers. It may surprise you that some states have laws that forbid asking the following information:

(1) Are you a U.S. citizen?
(2) What is your maiden name?
(3) If you speak a foreign language, you may not be asked how the language was learned.
(4) What is your draft status?

Obviously, most of the questions deal with national origin. Such questions are permissible, however, in case a bona fide occupational qualification is involved: for example, child labor laws; mandatory retirement ages; languages interpretation, government secret security clearance requiring citizenship.

How to Complete the Résumé—Before you begin any job seeking, you should prepare information—a résumé—on your education, training, and experience, so you can put your best foot forward and highlight your special talents.

The résumé should be brief, preferably one page, but certainly not more than two. Here is an example of a résumé with some helpful hints on preparing it:

JOHN R. ELLIS

Personal Data

Born 2/1/61   2018 Charleston Drive
Single—No dependents   Futura, Illinois
5'11"—175 lbs.   Phone (312) 439-9012

Education

1979—Graduated Futura High School, Futura, Illinois.
  Academic Course.
1981—Graduated Ritter Technical Institute, Cleveland, Ohio.
  Mechanical Technology (2 years).

Work Experience

Summer 1976   General work: mowed lawns and clerked in store.
Summer, 1978–79   Counselor, Camp Bradley, Pocono, Pennsylvania.
1980 to present   Stock clerk at Satellite Appliance Supply, Cleveland, Ohio, while attending school (21 hours per week).
                  (List military experience, if any.)

Miscellaneous Information

Member, Ritter Automotive Club.
Secretary, High School Science Club.
Have constructed own stereo set from spare parts.
2nd Class FCC radio-telephone license.
High School Honor Roll—two years.
Ritter Technical Institute Dean's List—one year.
Varsity baseball—high school.
Speaking knowledge of French.

Note the reference to the job—a stock clerk—in an appliance supply shop. It shows that despite working outside of class, you were able to make the Dean's List. Also, by building your own stereo set, you have shown that you are able to work with your hands besides being able to grasp theory in the classroom.

Furthermore, you show that you are a person with a wide variety of interests, what with participation in sports, the Automotive Club, and your knowledge of a second language.

COURTESY NEW JERSEY BELL TELEPHONE COMPANY

*An installer for New Jersey Bell brings phone service
into the home of a new subscriber.*

Here are some other tips in preparing and presenting the résumé:

(1) After you have organized your material and put it into the form you wish, it should be neatly typed. If it is not typed, the writing or printing should be neat and legible. If you are sending your résumé with a letter of application, or planning to hand it to an interviewer to read over, it is your first contact with your prospective employer.

(2) It is a rewarding idea to have your résumé typed on paper other than the usual white. A sheet of another color will be remembered longer by an employer, since almost all of the correspondence he receives is on white paper. Out of many résumés, he will remember the "blue one"—even though he may not know the name.

(3) You should send a short letter of application along with the résumé if you are applying for a job through the mail. If possible, learn the name of a specific person to whom the letter should be sent. If the information is not available, write to the employment manager or personnel manager.

(4) If applying for a job in person, take along several copies of your résumé, as it will save time during the interview. It will also indicate that you have planned your job hunting carefully. Even though the interviewer may ask you to complete an application, tell him you have prepared a résumé.

CHAPTER III

The Interview—from Both Sides of the Desk

This part of the job-hunting process is the "go–no-go" situation. This is the moment to which all of your preparations have led —your résumé—job application—job soliciting. I know of few places where anyone is hired without an interview of some sort—whether it be a single two-minute conversation or a detailed three- or four-hour process. The three- or four-hour interview would, of course, include testing, second interview, and so on.

To tell you not to be nervous during the interview would be to give you a sense of false security. Everyone is nervous in such situations —regardless of age, maturity, experience, or job level. It is the same with a professional athlete. Regardless of how many times he has played the game, he still gets butterflies each time he plays another. However, do not let the butterflies take over. Be master of yourself!

In all honesty, the interview is nothing more than a conversation. You must say something about yourself, for the interviewer needs to elicit as much information about you as he can, since he must match the proper person to the proper job. If he fails to do so, he may find he has a terminated employee on his hands. Then he will have to start the job-filling process all over again.

Remember, the fact that you are being interviewed means that some spark has been ignited in the mind of the employer. His time is valuable, and you have your foot in the door. Use your opportunity wisely.

ARRIVING AT THE EMPLOYMENT OFFICE

Some employment offices may be a cubicle with one chair, whereas others may be plush, carpeted, air-conditioned pads. In the latter you might find a receptionist, whereas in the cubicle type you might have to knock on the door for someone.

If no one greets you, be patient. Your attitude at this point could be a factor in getting the job. If a receptionist greets you, introduce yourself politely and state your business. You may have a prearranged appointment, in which case she will put you in contact with the interviewer. On the other hand, you may simply wish to inquire about positions and ask if you may have a copy of an employment application.

Many times the receptionist or secretary is the initial screener or the one to whom the actual interviewer may turn for an opinion. If you are polite and handle yourself well, she may make note of this to the interviewer.

Although personnel people are trained not to make judgments on first impressions, it is difficult to avoid doing so when one is confronted by an individual who is overbearing or has a surly attitude.

Dress and appearence do much to create first impressions. It is only common sense to assume that a young person—or any job applicant for that matter—will dress appropriately when appearing for an interview. Styles have changed so drastically during the last decade that it is almost impossible to offer guidelines on the proper attire for the interview. Dress in good taste—in simple style. This does not need to be a style dictated by the latest fashion.

Regardless of the type of job you are seeking, dress as you would for the best job in the organization. Wear that best outfit, for you will be judged against others who will be trying as hard as you are. Even if you are applying for a lower-level job, you will be remembered as the "applicant who was dressed properly."

If you must wait any length of time for the interviewer, browse through any literature that may be available in the waiting area. Further, you should have found out something about the firm before appearing for the interview—its size, what it manufactures, or what services it offers, its company officers, or even stock prices, if it is a large enough firm. Pamphlets or booklets in the waiting area may give you this type of information. Such bits of knowledge could come in handy during your discussion. You may be able to "sneak" some of them in—but don't give the impression of being a know-it-all.

Be prompt. Allow yourself plenty of time to arrive on the scene.

Take into consideration such emergencies as a flat tire, a slow train, or similar emergencies. Being late for an interview is inexcusable—except in case of an *extreme emergency*. If that happens—and it certainly is possible—phone the interviewer and inform him that you will be late. Or you can schedule another interview at the interviewer's convenience. This will show that you are a responsible person and have good judgment as well.

The applicant who arrives *too early* is a great burden to the personnel man. It is almost as bad as being late. Do not forget that he has a schedule to maintain, and the fact that you are sitting in the lobby can nag at him. When eventually you are interviewed this may cloud his thinking. A five-minute early arrival is sufficient. This will give you the time necessary to get the "lay of the land."

When you come face to face with the interviewer, introduce yourself in a clear voice. Offer to shake hands and do so with a firm handshake, not a "bone-crusher." The handshake is most important, for nothing gets an interview off to a poor start more rapidly than a tentative, lifeless handshake.

A gentleman is taught that it is not proper to shake hands with a lady unless she offers her hand first. It is proper—and sophisticated—to follow this rule. A lady's handshake should not be too firm. It should be—well—ladylike.

You must *never* chew gum during an interview. You should also refrain from smoking, as this might indicate nervousness. Everything must go well. Do not take chances.

The discussion will begin with "small talk" in order to get you relaxed and in a talking mood. This conversation will center around such topics as the weather, your trip to the office, a current news item, something on your application or résumé, such as sports, hobbies, or other special interests. Your answers to these casual questions will not mean as much as your answers will later in the interview, so do not be afraid to speak up. The interviewer wants you to talk, for he must get information.

Avoid plain "yes" or "no" answers. Your talking freely will allow the discussion to be more relaxed and will allow the interviewer to establish a friendly feeling of rapport with you.

Just do not become *too* friendly or *too* confident or you can blow the whole mood. There is a fine line between talking too much or talking too little.

The Search for Information

The prime responsibility of the interviewer when seeking qualified candidates is the search for information. The interviewer bases his decision upon the information you provide—both written and oral —on the application and at the interview. Not only will he seek out occupational information, but he will look for many personal traits. His questions will be directed toward obtaining that information. It is said that in a good interview, *you* will do 80 percent of the talking and the interviewer will do the other 20 percent.

The interviewer will discuss with you the answers you have given on the Employment Application. The sections of the Employment Application and how you should answer and treat them were handled in the preceding chapter. The interviewer will enlarge upon your answers in order to draw you out in more detail. As he is doing this, he will be attempting to discover the following things about you:

How you express yourself
The extent of your vocabulary
Your mannerisms
Your ability to "think on your feet"
Your sense of humor
Your basic temperament
Your ability to get along with others
He will also be looking for personal characteristics:

Positives	*Negatives*
Appearance	Gum chewing and/or smoking
Smile	Finger tapping
Politeness	Extreme nervousness
Sincerity	Shifting of the eyes
Humility	Avoidance of questions
Voice quality	Overaggressiveness
Methods of reasoning	Boastfulness
Intelligence	Talking yourself down
Patience	Adverse social attitude
	Antagonism
	Making excuses

When the interviewer is putting you at your ease or establishing a rapport with you, you can put your best foot forward in anticipating his questions. You can use the information you have given on the application as a basis for this anticipation. For example, if you had a part-time job and bought clothes for yourself with the money, say so. This will give him some indication of your responsibility, drive, and independence.

The question may arise as to whether you can type. If you can and have any experience, mention this, whether it was typing a thesis or working in the school office. This will reveal accuracy of typing, dependability, or the fact that you have worked in a regular office and know a certain amount of office procedure.

A simple question regarding a driver's license could lead to information telling the types of vehicles you have driven and can drive, your mechanical ability with tools.

A girl who is questioned about her manual dexterity and aptitude for fine work could mention special sewing she has done, artwork, clothes design, and other accomplishments in that general area.

In using this approach, you not only give the interviewer positive pointers about yourself, but you also display the quality of good oral expression and the fact that you are not shy or withdrawn.

While we are speaking of positive qualities, let us elaborate. The interviewer is seeking to hire a person who has the quality of being a group worker. At the same time, he is trying to avoid hiring a complainer, or an individual who cannot get along with or work with others. So avoid negatives. If you thought little of your last employer, do not emphasize or even mention it. Look at the good points of a firm.

To complain about your past employer or working conditions can indicate a lack of maturity and that you are a potential complainer. If you are asked a direct question, you will have to give an answer, but do so without misrepresenting yourself.

If conditions were not good at your previous job, you might answer in this way: "The working conditions were not good, but he did not have the necessary money or manpower to make things any better at the time. He can't be blamed entirely."

The interviewer, in an attempt to solicit as much information as possible, will ask questions in a special manner. He will avoid questions that lead to "yes" or "no" answers. For example, the same question can be asked in two ways:

Did you earn money during your summer vacations?
or
Describe the types of job you have had during the summer vacation periods.

The first question will bring an obvious "yes" or "no" answer, whereas the second is a search for information. Regardless of which one you are asked—lead the interviewer in the way we described. Do not answer with just a "yes" or "no," but grab the ball and take it from there.

In preparing for the interview, perhaps you can talk to someone who has been interviewed previously by the same company. You may be able to gain some insight into the type of questions that are asked or the temperament of the interviewer. It might help your nerves to have a bit of advance information. You may find that you know people in common or have a shared interest in sports or high school. However, do not become too informal. Be ambitious but *not* obnoxious.

After you have finished the interview, the interviewer will usually complete an Interviewer's Rating Form. He cannot rely fully upon his memory—especially if he talks to twenty or thirty people in one day. The next page shows a sample of such a form. Some rating forms may not be as detailed as this one, but you will get an idea of the depth of the questions he has asked.

Tips on Choosing an Interview Time

The timing of the interview can be a factor in getting the job or at least getting the proper audience. The time of day or the day of the week can be important. Even the sequence of your interview in relation to others applying for the same job is important.

1. The first person interviewed usually sets the standard for other applicants. If you know what your competition is, plan your interview time accordingly. If you know you are one of the best applicants, try to arrange an early interview. If you are an average candidate, gauge your time to be interviewed after a weaker candidate.

| INTERVIEWER'S REFERENCE FORM | APPLICANT'S NAME | | | | | POSITION APPLIED FOR | | DATE APPLIED |

I. PHYSICAL CHARACTERISTICS

TALL	HEAVY	NOTE ANY MANNERISMS OR CHARACTERISTICS OF APPLICANT AFFECTING ACCEPTANCE
MEDIUM	MEDIUM	
SHORT	THIN	

II. GENERAL CHARACTERISTICS (CHECK EACH REMARK)

APPEARANCE	GOOD	FAIR	POOR	EXPRESSIVE ABILITY	GOOD	FAIR	POOR	INTELLIGENCE	YES	NO
CLEANLINESS				VOICE QUALITY				FOLLOWS AND SHIFTS DISCUSSION QUICKLY		
NEATNESS				PRESENTATION-FLUENCY				RECOGNIZES VALUE OF OTHER VIEWPOINTS		
APPROP. APPAREL				PRESENTATION-COHERENCY				REASONING IS WELL FOUNDED		
				PRESENTATION-ORIGINALITY				QUESTIONS INTELLIGENT AND RELATED		

PERSONALITY TRAITS (CHECK ONLY THOSE WHICH APPLY)

| WITHDRAWN, SHY, UNDULY NERVOUS | UNDERRATES SELF | MISREPRESENTED SELF IN APPLICATION |
| OVERLY AGGRESSIVE, FORCEFUL | OVERRATES SELF | |

III. WORK HISTORY (CHECK ONLY IF ANSWER IS YES)

OBTAINED HIS OWN JOBS	HAD JUSTIFIABLE REASON FOR LEAVING
PROGRESSED SATISFACTORILY	PREVIOUS EXPERIENCE WILL BE OF:
SHOWED STABILITY	MINOR VALUE MAJOR VALUE

IV. FAMILY AND DOMESTIC

| WIFE IS WORKING | OWNS HIS HOME | HAS OTHER INCOME |
| DESIRES WIFE TO WORK | WILLING TO RELOCATE | HAS SAVINGS ACCOUNT |

V. JOB MOTIVE

	MAJ.	MIN.	NONE		MAJ.	MIN.	NONE
IN NEED OF WORK				OPPORTUNITY FOR SPECIALIZED TRAINING			
INCREASED INCOME				JUST OUT OF CURIOSITY			
OPPORTUNITY FOR ADVANCEMENT				PUSHED INTO IT BY FAMILY			
TO ENTER NEW FIELD							

VI. SOCIAL ADJUSTMENT (CHECK ONLY WHERE APPLICABLE)

| ATTITUDE TOWARD PEOPLE IN GENERAL | ADVERSE SOCIAL ATTITUDE AFFECTING ACCEPTANCE | INTERESTED IN CURRENT EVENTS AND CIVIC AFFAIRS | HAS DIVERSIFIED INTERESTS |
| FRIENDLY   RESERVED   ANTAGONISTIC | | | |

VII. TECHNICAL INTERVIEW

							YES	NO
1. TEST	SCORE	3. TEST	SCORE	5. TEST	SCORE	ADEQUATE KNOWLEDGE FOR POSITION		
						KNOWLEDGE COMPARABLE WITH BACKGROUND		
2.		4.		6.		WEAK IN THEORY		
						WEAK IN PRACTICAL ASPECT		

VIII. INTERVIEWS

| INTERVIEWER | DATE | ACCEPTABILITY   YES   NO   DOUBTFUL |
| COMMENTS: | | |

| INTERVIEWER | DATE | ACCEPTABILITY   YES   NO   DOUBTFUL |
| COMMENTS: | | |

IX. RECOMMENDED DISPOSITION

This choosing of your own time may be difficult unless you sign up for an interview ahead of time. An example of this might be interviews given to college seniors on campus. If such is the case, you might be able to slot yourself conveniently between two candidates who are less qualified than you:

If you feel you are a weak candidate, being first may not hurt you because by the end of the day, when the interviewer looks over his rating sheets, you may seem more like an average candidate than a weak one. By being first, he has seen no one before you to use as a standard.

2. Try to avoid the first interview on a Monday morning. This is usually the busiest time of the week in any establishment, whether it be a factory, store, finance office, or wherever. It is also true for the interviewer. The weekend is an American tradition and late Friday assignments are often put off until Monday morning. You may not have a choice, but if it can be arranged, take a time other than Monday morning.

Try to avoid interviews immediately before lunch or near closing time. Again, it is human nature, but an interviewer who skipped breakfast or is in a hurry to get home may not give you the consideration you deserve.

3. Friday can be a good day for an interview, especially during the morning. Experience shows that this is the day with the least number of scheduled interviews: both applicant and interviewer are probably getting ready for the weekend. As a result, more people are scheduled for Monday. Most firms run employment ads on the weekend. By applying on Friday, you may be able to get the jump on a job that has not yet been listed in the paper. However, it is suggested that you avoid late Friday interviews or late hours before a holiday. That long weekend rears its head.

4. How about *your* "peak" period of the day? Most of us have a time when we function and perform especially well. If possible, schedule your interview accordingly. It is especially important if tests are to be administered.

TRADE SECRETS OF THE INTERVIEW

I hope I have not described the interview as a mystery story with a cloak-and-dagger atmosphere. It is no more than a two-way conversation that attempts to match a job vacancy to someone seeking a job.

The employment interviewer is trained to uncover information that will help to make this matching of requirement and talent come more easily. Let us look at some of his techniques.

The *rapport* aspect or loosening-up process was described earlier as the technique of getting you to talk while he listened for key points from you—whether it be overselling or underselling.

He will use special methods to obtain this information. For example, he may change the conversation in the middle of a sentence to find how agile your mind is—how well you "think on your feet."

If, when an interviewer asks a question, the applicant asks if he may smoke or lights a pipe, the interviewer knows that he is stalling for time to think out an answer. Another trick under the same circumstances is for a person to drop a pencil or handkerchief. In those instances, an experienced interviewer will usually switch the conversation to another angle, since he is familiar with this ploy. It would be well not to employ such tactics.

Although the following technique would not be used with teenagers, it is worth noting. This technique is called the *stress* interview. The methods used seek to discover the extent of one's poise and stability. To do this, the interviewer may purposely create a feeling of tension or antagonism to see how well the applicant keeps his composure in the situation.

In order to arrive at an evaluaton of the traits of adaptability or intelligence, the interviewer may present many facts and details to you to which he may refer later in the interview. In such a case you must stay alert and listen to his every word rather than thinking of what your reply is going to be. You might even ask if you may take a few notes, since the information is interesting and you would like to keep it for future reference. Jotting down notes should fix the information more firmly in your mind.

It is suggested that you do not talk to the interviewer from notes you have written before the interview. This can show a lack of self-confidence. Any information pertaining to the interview should be memorized.

If you have brought along samples of work that you think might be of particular interest, do not be anxious to display them. Early in the interview, mention that you have the samples and are prepared to show them. Wait until you are asked before you open your briefcase. Interviewers can become aggravated with the person who clutters the desk with diplomas, certificates, citations, commendations, letters of recommendation, medals, photographs. Such displays can make a person seem overly aggressive to the point of being "pushy."

In order to make you show some quality of patience, the interviewer may keep you waiting before the discussion or purposely delay during the talk. This situation will not be common with the teenage interview. However, necessary interruptions may occur. Do not display any impatience or displeasure if that happens.

The interviewer's time is usually at a premium, and you should not be too "gabby" with your answers. He may interpret lengthy answers as a trait of being talkative, which in turn can be translated into job performance or a lack thereof. You can actually practice the interview and have prepared answers on those questions that are normally asked. Use answers that do not ramble; employ a good vocabulary and logic.

In Chapter II, the various sections of the Employment Application were described in detail. Use these as the basis for questions. Other typical questions that might be asked are:

Why do you want to work for our firm?
What are your short/long range job plans?
What do you do with the money you earn?
What do you want to do when you finish high school/college?

If you have access to a tape recorder, practice hearing yourself speak. You will be surprised at such things as pauses in your speech, stuttering, repeated use of the same words, inflections in your voice. They are important to correct, since the interviewer will quickly detect those and other mannerisms.

Watch such points as slouching in your chair, shifting of your eyes from the speaker, fidgeting, nervously fingering objects, too much gesturing with the hands and arms . . . these can be red flags to the interviewer—yet they may not really be you. You may simply be nervous in this new situation.

Evaluating Personal Traits

Earlier in this chapter an Interviewer's Rating Form was presented that described the various qualities he seeks during the interview. In order to provide greater insight into this phase of the interview, the next pages depict a rating scale devised by the Small Business Administration for a self-evaluation of personal traits. It could really serve as an interviewer's form, since he is attempting to discover these same traits during the interview. Be honest with yourself in checking the various sections.

The Secondary Interview

In large firms, or with jobs that require a special skill, you can expect an interview beyond the Personnel Office. This discussion will mainly deal with your technical background rather than personal qualities. The fact that you are being referred for a second interview means that you are over several hurdles—the initial screening and the testing phase.

The person who will conduct this secondary interview will probe into your ability actually to perform the job. He will also try to determine how well you would fit into his group or "team." He will have in front of him your completed application and the remarks from the personnel man.

Do not be hesitant to ask about the special aspects of the job. You can even request a tour of the facilities and work area if it is possible. It could be that tours are not given because of restricted areas, government work, or similar reasons. If it cannot be granted, it will nevertheless display a keen interest on your part.

Closing the Interview

In closing the interview you can expect one of the following statements:

(1) You do not qualify for the position.
(2) You do qualify and will be offered a job on the spot or in writing.
(3) You do qualify, but cannot be given an answer at this time. (Other candidates may be under consideration, or the person who conducted the secondary interview must be consulted.)

If the issue is still open, be sure to determine who will make the next contact—you or the employer—and when.

If an employment offer is made or is forthcoming—and you want the job:

Instructions: Place a check mark on the line following each trait where you think the mark ought to be. The check mark need not be placed directly over one of the guide phrases, because the rating may lie somewhere between the phrases.

INITIATIVE			
Additional tasks sought; highly ingenious	Resourceful; alert to opportunities	Regular work performed without waiting for directions	Routine work awaiting directions
ATTITUDE TOWARD OTHERS			
Positive; friendly interest in people	Pleasant, polite	Sometimes difficult to work with	Inclined to be quarrelsome or uncooperative
LEADERSHIP			
Forceful, inspiring confidence and loyalty	Order giver	Driver	Weak
RESPONSIBILITY			
Responsibility sought and welcomed	Accepted without protest	Unwilling to assume without protest	Avoided whenever possible

ORGANIZING ABILITY	Highly capable of perceiving and arranging fundamentals in logical order	Able organizer	Fairly capable of organizing	Poor organizer
INDUSTRY	Industrious; capable of working hard for long hours	Can work hard, but not for too long a period	Fairly industrious	Hard work avoided
DECISION	Quick and accurate	Good and careful	Quick, but often unsound	Hesitant and fearful
SINCERITY	Courageous, square shooter	On the level	Fairly sincere	Inclined to lack sincerity
PERSEVERANCE	Highly steadfast in purpose; not discouraged by obstacles	Effort steadily maintained	Average determination and persistence	Little or no persistence
PHYSICAL ENERGY	Highly energetic at all times	Energetic most of time	Fairly energetic	Below average

(1) Establish a date when you will report to work.
(2) What type of clothing you will need to wear if it is a special job.
(3) The hours of employment.
(4) Learn what the eating facilities are.

It would be regrettable if you did not carry your lunch the first day and discovered that no lunch facilities existed on the premises. If you are still a teenager, missing a meal could be a disaster.

If an employment offer is not extended, you might ask a few tactful questions as to why you were not selected. The answers can be helpful during your next interview.

Above all else—*don't be discouraged if you don't connect on your first or second interview.* You have learned something for the next one.

The Exit Interview

The exit interview is a special type of interview that deals with employees who are *leaving* a particular firm. The purpose of this interview is to provide clearance on such items as final pay, tools and equipment, security debriefing, extension or elimination of employee benefits, and a most important phase of employment: to learn your reason for leaving and to get your impressions of the firm. In a sense, it might be considered an attitude survey. Most larger firms conduct these interviews faithfully or will forward a questionnaire for the employee to complete and return by mail.

This is good personnel practice, for comments of terminating employees can be more valid than those of present employees, since those departing no longer have a vested right in the firm. Reduction of turnover and favorable change of policies can develop from these comments. Firms who do not correctly interpret comments of separating employees can expect greater employee relations problems.

Most teenagers who receive this type of separation interview will not be confronted with the attitude-survey phase of the process. Mostly, they will be leaving a job to go back to school.

If you are given this opportunity, however, be careful not to burn your bridges behind you. If you have had unfavorable experiences, determine how your information will be interpreted before you willingly give unfavorable data.

On the positive side, keep the door open for your return to the firm, especially if you were employed part-time or during the summer. Leave a favorable impression. You will want to use this employer as a reference. Leave addresses where you can be reached for a job next summer—or perhaps a part-time job at Christmas.

CHAPTER IV

Employment Tests: What Tests to Expect and How to Take Them

Afraid to take tests?

You should not be, since certain techniques can give you self-assurance in getting you over one of the major hurdles of the job-hunting process.

As you may recall, it was mentioned earlier that the most important part of the job hunt is the interview. You will know that they have seen something they liked during the interview if you are asked to take various selection tests. Do not drop the ball at this phase of the process.

This chapter will deal with various types of preemployment tests, how to take them, and how the personnel man interprets them.

The purpose of employment tests is mainly to determine whether you have certain aptitudes, interests, and ability to perform a job. Further, they tend to measure whether you have the necessary skills and training and—in the case of personality tests—to find out whether you can fit into the organization. The employer finds testing very useful—and necessary.

A poorly selected employee can be costly in bad workmanship as well as turnover if it becomes necessary to terminate him. Also, if an employee becomes dissatisfied, he may quit the organization. He might quit the organization because he is unqualified for the job—or because he is overqualified. Those things should be discovered before he is hired. More of this later.

Many employees require long training periods, and it may be some time before they become fully productive and "earn their keep." While learning, they contribute little to an organization, and this is an added cost. If during or after this training period, they should leave or are fired, all of the original investment is lost to the employer. The employee has lost, too, because he must begin job hunting again.

The idea of being *too qualified* for a job sounds strange, doesn't it? It is a proven fact that people who are too well qualified become unhappy and leave. Take the case of a secretary in a pure typing or filing job who takes little or no dictation. The job is interesting at first, but she quickly realizes that she is not utilizing her shorthand and becomes bored with the routine typing and filing.

How about the fellow who has acquired a skill in the Vocational-Technical School (electronic technician or appliances serviceman) and accepts a simple electronic assembly job. He won't be happy for long.

The fact that you overqualify for the job could be revealed by your scoring too well on the exam—one that might be too simple and far below your level of education and training.

An employer may not use tests and simply offer you a lower-level job. It is true that perhaps you may not get the job you want immediately—but be careful what you choose.

I have been speaking mainly of industrial tests. The same principles apply to other types of tests as well—college entrance exams and armed forces tests, for example. Here again, it is a matter of proper placement, or the organization has lost time, money, and energy in acquiring you. You have lost the same.

What types of test can you expect in job hunting, in going on to further schooling, or in other pursuits?

Intelligence Test

Probably the most common test is the one measuring "intelligence." This type of test may be labeled by other names: test of "adaptability"; "ability to adjust to new situations"; "capacity to learn"; "IQ." In a nutshell, the purpose of the test is to measure your capacity to learn and to perform a required job, task, or undertake a period of learning.

In being measured for this quality, you should expect questions dealing with the following:

Number Analogies

"2 is to 4 as 4 is to ?"
(This is a level of simple reasoning.)

Series of Numbers

"1 – 3 – ? – 7 – 9"

(Again—a level of reasoning to determine a pattern of numbers.)

Word Analogies

"Hot is to cold as black is to ? "

(A matter of opposites.)

Spatial Relations

"This   is to   as   is to __ "
(a)   (b)   (c)   (d)

(This is a case of visualization of geometric forms—
a third-dimension concept.)

Mathematics

"How many 3¢ stamps in a dozen?"
"If eggs are 12¢ a dozen, how many will $1.00 buy?"

Vocabulary

"criticize—praise"
(Opposites or the same?)
"Which word does not belong in the group?"
Apple—banana—carrot—lemon—berry
(Determination between fruits and a vegetable.)

These are basic and simple examples. However, as you progress
with the test, the questions will become increasingly difficult. You
may not be able to answer some of the questions. This is expected
in most tests.

Intelligence tests are generally "power" tests; they become more
difficult as the exam progresses and measure all levels of intelligence.
It takes an exceptional individual to complete an intelligence test
in a given time and get all the answers correct. I will dwell on this
point later when describing techniques given on these power tests.

When applying for industrial jobs, you can expect short intelligence tests of twelve to thirty minutes in length. You can expect longer and more complicated tests for admission to schools beyond high school—the armed forces or for training in specialized occupations. However, the same general type of questions will be used. Industry uses the shorter forms because they are easier to administer and can be scored more quickly. The tests are usually scored while you are in the office.

Your score will be measured against "norms," or how you have scored in relation to others who have taken the tests. These can be norms of the general population, high-school graduates, or simply how your score compares with employees of the firm where you are applying.

Tests of Mechanical Aptitude or Ability

These tests will be administered to those individuals seeking positions involving such occupations as assembler, laboratory assistant, electronic technician, appliance serviceman, auto mechanic, engineering student, computer repairman, truck driver.

You can expect a simple test of assembling a small instrument—a lock or bell—or assembling nuts and bolts, or placing various geometric forms into receptacles in which they fit properly (pegboards, wiggly blocks), tweezer usage, tracing a maze.

These tests tend to measure:

(1) Depth of dexterity
(2) Motor coordination
(3) Visual discrimination
(4) Spatial relations (three dimensions)

In addition to the above, when applying for a skilled or semi-skilled job, other factors will be considered, such as limitations of physical endurance, coordination with hand tools, do you like getting dirty.

Spatial relations are a big factor. It is difficult to describe the quality. It concerns itself mainly with visualizing third dimension (depth). This measures the ability to notice size and shape of figures and to differentiate among small differences. It involves a kind of retention for geometric figures and the ability to visualize them in various positions.

Some of the occupations to be considered here are not only assembly positions, but engineering (blueprint reading and mechanical drawing), dentistry (working with mirrors and at odd angles), artistry (giving feeling of depth in paintings).

Aptitude Tests

The basic purpose of an aptitude test is to measure potential. Aptitude is a present condition thought to indicate what the potentialities can be.

The tests are built upon a person's inherent qualities, and not upon experiences. Aptitude tests do not directly measure future accomplishment, but provide an indication of the potentialities.

Present performance can be a measure of this probability. High-school grades can be a fairly good indication of whether you can complete college or other higher learning. This stresses the importance of high-school transcripts.

Further, if you achieved well in high school in a given area with very little effort, that is a good sign of having the aptitude for this particular area.

Various types of aptitude tests are:

Scientific	Medicine/Dentistry
Clerical	Teaching
Law (reasoning)	Music
Language aptitude	Art
Verbal	

Interest Inventories

These questionnaires are not considered tests since you are required to list a preference. A preference is an individual "thing" and cannot be considered as right or wrong. When you are given many choices to make, then the results tend to show the similarity between your interests and those of persons in particular occupations.

For example, you can expect questions as to whether you like to

play a musical instrument.
browse through a bookstore.
play a game of baseball.

After answering a hundred or so of these questions, you can see that the pattern of your interests will develop.

The Kuder Preference Record by Science Research Associates is a well-known interest inventory and is aimed at measuring your interests and preferences. Individual interests are broken down into the following categories:

COURTESY BUCKS COUNTY TECHNICAL SCHOOL
FAIRLESS HILLS, PENNSYLVANIA

Entrance to the Technical School requires specific aptitudes.

Mechanical	Artistic
Computational	Literary
Scientific	Musical
Persuasive	Social service

Clerical

Some tips for the taking:

Be consistent with your choices, for the test may be designed to determine your "truthfulness." Do not try to "outguess" the test or yourself. Choose your true interest or the one that most closely suits you.

A point of interest. You may have strong inclinations in an area and yet not have the aptitude for such work. A complete battery of tests will bring this out. Such conflicts (interest versus aptitude), if not discovered early, lead to choosing the wrong vocation and eventual job failure.

Opinions vary among psychologists, counselors, and others directly involved with testing as to whether an individual is born with certain aptitudes or can acquire them.

My personal opinion is that it is a combination of factors. Your early childhood training and environment can do much to develop potential in a given area.

Let us review two areas: mechanical leanings and sports. Many people have had these "talents" cultivated by parental influence or some other outside factor. For example, the person who was raised on a farm and had to turn his hand to all the problems that arise there might easily have developed an aptitude for mechanical skills. He most certainly would have developed muscles in the process. A person who was uncoordinated in his early years, but had the good fortune to be born into an athletic family, would certainly develop his athletic potential as he grew.

What do you think?

GENERAL APTITUDE TEST BATTERY (GATB)

One of the most valued and widely used series of aptitude tests is the General Aptitude Test Battery (GATB) administered by the Bureau of Employment section of the Department of Labor and Industry. This program is conducted through the various State Employment Services (SES). School counselors know of this free testing series and often refer people to it.

This group of tests consists of twelve separate sections. Some are "paper-and-pencil" tests, others are of the mechanical aptitude variety. The tests aim to measure potential abilities and aptitude in nine areas. The nine areas are described in the following information taken from the Bureau of Employment Security literature.

The aptitude tests are designed to measure capacities to *learn* various jobs. Although such selection devices are already in use for a large variety of occupations, many occupational areas are not covered. When a need arises for test-measuring one of those areas, the USES (United States Employment Service), in cooperation with the appropriate State Employment Service, develops a tailor-made set of tests to meet that need. The process of developing such a set of tests—or aptitude test battery—requires a certain cooperation from the employer who is interested in getting test-selected applicants for a particular occupation.

Definitions of Aptitudes Measured

Intelligence—General learning ability. The ability to "catch on" or understand instructions and underlying principles; the ability to reason and make judgments. Closely related to doing well in school.

Verbal Aptitude—The ability to understand meanings of words and the ideas associated with them—and to use them effectively.

COURTESY MARIE H. KATZENBACH SCHOOL FOR THE DEAF
WEST TRENTON, NEW JERSEY

The vocational school provides for the development of salable skills.

The ability to comprehend language, to understand relationships between words, and to understand meanings of whole sentences and paragraphs. The ability to present information or ideas clearly.

Numerical Aptitude—Ability to perform arithmetic operations quickly and accurately.

Spatial Aptitude—Ability to think visually of geometric forms and to comprehend the two-dimensional representation of three-dimensional objects. The ability to recognize the relationships resulting from the movement of objects in space.

Form Perception—Ability to perceive pertinent detail in objects or in pictorial or graphic material. Ability to make visual comparisons and discriminations, and see slight differences in shapes and shadings of figures, and widths and lengths of lines.

Clerical Perception—Ability to perceive pertinent detail in verbal tabular material. Ability to observe differences in copy, to proofread words and numbers, and to avoid perceptual errors in arithmetic computation.

COURTESY U.S. DEPARTMENT OF LABOR

The pegboard test measures degrees of manual dexterity that are needed to become proficient in certain occupations.

Motor Coordination—Ability to coordinate eyes and hands or fingers rapidly and accurately in making precise movements with speed. Ability to make a movement response accurately and swiftly. Probably related to reaction time.

Finger Dexterity—Ability to move the fingers, and manipulate small objects with the fingers, rapidly and accurately.

Manual Dexterity—Ability to move the hands easily and skillfully. Ability to work with the hands in placing and turning motions.

Anyone can take the tests. Although they are generally administered to persons seeking a job for the first time, they are also used to determine ability in those who want to or must change to a line of work in which they have had no experience. They are also used for those who are considering some type of vocational training.

Special Aptitude Tests

Many specialized aptitude tests are available when specific qualities are being sought. You may not be exposed to this upon graduation or in the early stages of your work career, but I should mention a few.

Probably the most famous specialized tests are the Seashore Music Tests, which measure such musical qualities as:

Sense of pitch	Rhythmic action	Acuity of hearing
Sense of intensity	Register of voice	Voice control
Sense of time	Tonal memory	Singing on key

Such questionnaires are not only concerned with the music field, but can measure qualities for such other occupations as the communications field or similar areas in which hearing acuity and sound discrimination are needed.

Other tests measure aptitude in physics, chemistry, mathematics, English, sales, or foreign languages. The foreign language test is interesting in that it deals with an artificial language in relation to grammar, language inference, and language construction.

Clerical Tests

Clerical tests are usually administered to individuals seeking positions as secretaries, keypunch operators, file clerks, computer operators, banking positions, accounting clerks, statistical analysts, and other positions involving mathematics or clerical procedures.

You can expect items such as:

Number Checking $6584 vs. 6584
                       89.88 vs. 88.98
                       (like and unlike items)
Fractions and Percentages   25 percent of 8 is __
                       1/12 =   .0 .

Word Problems   If $500 is deposited in a bank at 4 percent
                             interest compounded annually, what is the
                             balance after two years?
Word Checking   Robert L. Keefe vs. Robert I. Keefe
Alphabetizing   Place in the correct alphabetical order:
                             occipital, occasion, occlude, ocelot.

Most of these will be timed tests:

TYPING

This will involve your speed as well as accuracy. There must be a proper balance between the two. It depends upon the job. However, most employers seem to prefer a slower, more accurate typist to the person who works rapidly but makes many mistakes.

In addition to straight typing, you may receive a test wherein you must retype a letter draft that has been corrected. It would be something like this:

"This is to inform you of our interest in your fine background

                             u
in clerical skills. I wish to persue the matter further and & would

                  an   P.M.
like you to appear for interview Friday at 2:30   "

You can also expect typing tests dealing with numbers—especially columns of figures requiring alignment and correction.

A word of caution: Be prepared to take a typing test on a manual typewriter rather than the electric variety. The last girl hired in the office usually gets the oldest typewriter, and it may not be electric. This is usually the exception, however. It is best to be proficient with the electric machine, but be prepared for this.

In addition, ask whether you may practice on the test typewriter for a few minutes before taking the test. You can get the feel of the machine before the exam.

Most offices do not give a test on other office machines. However, if you have other machines marked on your application or your résumé, be prepared in case you are asked.

SHORTHAND TEST

This test will usually be administered by a record or simply by direct dictation. Results here will measure:

(1) The ability to transcribe
(2) The form of the letter you type
(3) Typing ability
(4) Spelling
(5) Grammar

If you receive dictation from a person, feel free to ask him to repeat a word if you miss it. In this type of dictation, you will usually find that it will be slower than the record, for there is a tendency on the part of the individual to slow his pace if he sees that you are falling behind. Also, he may want to collect his thoughts if he is not reading the dictation.

In transcribing, do not leave blank spaces if you have missed a word. Be resourceful and fill in with one of your own. However, be sure that the word makes sense and parallels the rest of the sentence. When the test is corrected, the new word may not be noticed, whereas a blank space jumps out at the reader.

PERSONALITY OR ADJUSTMENT TESTS

These really are not tests as such, but again, questionnaires or inventories. Their main purpose is to determine whether you have the personal qualities or characteristics for a given position. In other words, do you fit the pattern for working with others in the same classification?

These tests will measure such factors as:

Cooperation	Adjustment
Aggressiveness	Masculinity
General activity	Nervous tendencies
Extraversion/Introversion	

The inventories are usually longer than most others, but are normally one statement, easily read and requiring a simple "yes" or "no" answer.

Here are sample questions:

> "Are you afraid to take tests?"
> "Are you reluctant to speak up in a group?"
> "Are you afraid to make mistakes?"
> "Do you consider yourself a fast worker?"
> "Are you impatient with slow workers?"
> "Do you feel that you have more good days than bad days?"

You can see what is being measured. Do not attempt to "slant" the test because there may be duplicate questions that are phrased differently, and you will have to recall your previous answers.

As you read this chapter, we hope you will be able to visualize what picture the tests are attempting to portray. When scored and placed in a "profile," the employer, school, or organization has some idea of your intelligence, aptitude, interests, and abilities.

The scores and pattern will be compared with other individuals in a similar situation and a decision made. This comparison can be made with employees on the job, students enrolled at the school, etc.

TECHNIQUES ON HOW TO TAKE A TEST

People who are quite capable of passing tests often will fail them. Many times it happens because they are not versed in how to approach the situation. This section will deal with tips on how to take a test in order to score more successfully.

Attitude—Time of Day—Health

All these factors are mportant, and if you have control over them, you will benefit greatly.

Time of day is important because we all have "peak" periods when we operate more efficiently. If possible, arrange to take the test during the time when you are sharpest.

Get plenty of rest—be alert rather than in a stupor because of lack of sleep. Relax before the test—do not get there at the last minute.

If materials are required for the exam—pencils, papers, erasers, pens, slide rule—bring these as well as adequate supplies to provide for emergencies. This will be important if the test is timed. Not having an extra pencil on a timed test can really knock points from a score.

If you have a choice of where to sit, take into consideration such factors as light, noise, place in the room. Are you close enough to hear well? Can you see?

If you are to be exposed to the tests for a prolonged period without a break, take along a candy bar or some other type of food to pick you up. I am speaking here of the occasion when there may be three or four hours of concentrated testing.

Test Preparation—How to Study

You may not be able to prepare for many tests—especially aptitude or interest inventories. An achievement test, however, is a horse of a different color, and you should review your time schedule and plan accordingly.

It is best not to cram, but review well in advance. A final examination cannot be studied for in one night. You need to review a whole year's work on a regular basis in order to be fully prepared.

Determine whether you can get sample tests ahead of time. Get a feel for the types of question to be asked. Find out whether it will be a timed test and how it will be scored.

Have someone else quiz you on the material to be covered. If others are taking the same test, get together and discuss possible questions that might be asked. Take advantage of this time, however; do not make it into a bull session.

Let us look at the tests themselves and the various approaches to taking them:

Read the directions carefully and ask any questions you may have on what is expected.

1. Is it a timed test? If so, what is the time limit? Will there be any warning given before the end of the test? Wear a watch to help you gauge your time. There may be a wall clock for your use.

If the test contains more than one question, find out if the various sections are to be timed separately. Further, can you go on to the next section if you have finished the others? This may be important, since some sections are sure to be more difficult for you than others.

2. What test aids are you allowed to use: scratch paper, slide rule, math tables?

3. Look at the entire test before jumping in. There will usually be directions on how to approach the exam. Directions usually tell:

(1) Time limit
(2) How to mark your answers
(3) Sample questions
(4) How to approach the questions (not spending too much time on one item, but moving on).

The proper way the answer is to be marked is very important. You must determine whether it is done on the test or on an answer sheet. Determine what type of mark is to be made and ask whether the answers are to be hand-scored or machine-scored.

If the test is to be mechanically scored, do not rest your pencil on the paper between questions. The machine may pick this up, and you will receive credit for wrong answers. If you decide to change an answer, be sure to erase thoroughly. The machine may pick up an incomplete erasure.

Complete all of the sample questions in order to get the idea of the test. The samples are normally very easy, in order to give you insight into the type of questions and how to mark them. Also, the simplicity of the questions will bolster your ego and help you to relax. You can expect three or four such questions.

Let us review the most important aspects of the process—the actual answering of the questions. Various types of test each require unique approaches, and you can expect to score better by observing the following points:

True-False Test

Making one of two choices—true or false—is not as easy as it sounds.

You should attempt to find out how the test will be scored. It may not be a simple matter of the number wrong and the number correct.

For example, if on a traditional test of 10 questions you have a total of 7 correct answers, you will usually receive a score of 70. However, on a true-false test, the number of *wrong* answers is *subtracted* from your total of correct answers. In this instance, your score would be 40 (7 correct answers minus 3 wrong ones = 4). Why? Because there is a possibility of your guessing correctly, since you have only two choices. The correct answers minus the wrong answers introduce the equalizing factor.

As a result, in this type of test, it is advantageous not to answer a question at all rather than to guess. It may save you points.

Be extremely careful of the wording on true-false questions. The question is either *true* or *false* and certain words can make them so. Watch such all-inclusive words as "never," "always," "all," "forever," and superlatives such as "highest," "smallest," "fastest." In order for a statement to be true or false, an absolute condition must exist when these words are used.

An example:

"The sun always shines in Arizona." The temptation is to answer this with "true." But how about the rainy days? and every night?

Multiple-Choice Questions

This type of question allows you to make a choice from three, four, or five possible answers. I say "possible" since none of the answers that are given may be correct. Look at this:

Eighty (80) divided by two (2) is

(a) 4.0
(b) 400
(c) .40
(d) none of the above

Of course the answer is (d).

I have given this example with other thoughts in mind: You must read all questions carefully. What does the question really ask and what is the answer? This is the type of question you can read too quickly and be tempted to answer with (a) or (c).

On the other hand, if you were faced with the following question:

Eighty (80) divided by two (2) is

> (a) 40
> (b) 20
> (c) 400
> (d) 4.0

You obviously know that (a) is the answer and you need not read further. This can be a timesaver, but be absolutely sure if you use this approach.

Again, determine how multiple-choice tests will be scored. Is guessing worth the chance?—It may be.

In multiple-choice tests, other formulae are used as equalizers. These are not as drastic as the true-false questions, because there is less chance for guessing.

Scoring is normally effected by using the formula of "Right minus the fraction of one less than the number of choices." If there are four choices, the formula would be "4 choices—right minus ⅓ wrong"; "5 choices—right minus ¼ wrong"; etc. If you receive 80 correct and 20 wrong on a test of 100 questions on a 5-choice question test, your score would be right minus ¼ wrong, or $80 - 5 = 75$ percent. The same score on a true-false test would be $80 - 20$ or 60 percent.

In summary, it will be necessary for you to (1) study the question to decide what it really asks; (2) scrutinize the choices and eliminate the obviously wrong answers; (3) make the proper choice. Since guessing is not an extreme penalty with four or five answers, an "educated guess" might be worth the risk.

Completion Questions

These types are most difficult to answer because you must know the absolute answer—or make a very good guess.

A type of completion question would be the following:

> "A famous Civil War Union general who became President of the United States was ＿＿＿＿＿ ＿＿ ＿＿＿＿＿＿＿＿."

Key points to keep in mind with this type of question are:

(1) Can you guess, and will there be any special penalties for a wrong answer? Many times, there is no special penalty, and the answer will be counted wrong whether you answer it incorrectly or

offer no answer at all. The total point score will be the number of questions correct. It is safe to guess in this instance.

(2) Many times the number of spaces in the answer will be a clue to the proper words. The test pattern will tell you. In the example above, the answer is a three-word name, and a correct guess would be Ulysses S. Grant.

Also, looking closely at subject-verb agreement will help you with the answer. A plural verb will take a plural answer. The type of article preceding a word may be helpful, also: a, an, or, the.

Matching Questions

This type of question concerns itself with matching one column of words with another. The answer column will usually contain more words than the question column in order to avoid simple matching by the process of elimination. However, some tests provide for using the same answer several times. If the directions do not tell you this, it is wise to ask before beginning.

Question	Answer
__ 25 percent	1/3
__ 50 percent	1/4
__ 440 yds.	1/2
__ 2 quarts	2/3
__ 2 pecks	1/5

Again, guessing here will not usually penalize since the number correct is the score.

Essay Questions

This type of question is one designed to determine how well you know a specific subject and how well you can organize your thoughts in expressing your answer. Here you must know your subject and there are no choices as with the above sections.

Do not approach a question of this type too hurriedly—it usually carries more points than other sections of the test.

Words of Advice

(1) Read the question carefully to determine what is being sought. Is an outline required? Is the answer to be detailed? Are dates and other factual information needed? Are you to make a comparison? Are you to develop something?

(2) If you are allowed to have scratch paper, jot down an outline or important facts about the question. Gather your information before you begin writing.

(3) The length of your answer may help you, provided you say something, or if the person scoring considers a weighty answer in ounces.

(4) Use a topic sentence and attempt to give the most important point of your answer in the first paragraph. This is a good beginning: develop it from there. Perhaps the scorer may not be at his mental or physical best when marking the test and may only scan the remainder of the answer after reading a good beginning.

(5) Underline key words in your answer. If the scorer follows the underlined words, he will quickly find the answers he is seeking.

(6) Give specific examples where possible in order to illustrate or to fortify your answer.

(7) Good punctuation and grammar are taken for granted. An otherwise accurate answer can be weakened by misspelling and bad constructions.

Other Tips

I want to stress again the importance of reading the test directions carefully, knowing if possible how the test is to be scored, and planning your approach. In regard to the last point, do not spend too much time on one question; go on to the next one and return later to those you have not answered. Although the most difficult questions are found near the end of most tests, you may be able to answer some or most of them. As mentioned earlier, most tests are scored based upon the number you have answered corectly. Answer first those questions you are sure of. If you have enough time to go over the unanswered questions, then do your guessing.

Good luck!

CHAPTER V

Summer Jobs and Part-Time Jobs

Almost every person in his teenage years has held a summer job or a part-time job, either between school terms, before college, or just as a stopgap while waiting for something else to happen.

Such jobs are probably the most commonly held positions and can be easier to come by if you know the techniques of job hunting. Or they can be the most difficult jobs to find because you must make a bid within a given time or lose the opportunity for the summer. Once summer jobs are filled, it can be almost impossible to find an extra one lying around loose.

In addition to the time element within which you must operate, the competition is much greater because there are usually many more applicants than jobs.

So you must know when to look, how to look, and where to look for the right job.

Types of Summer Job

Summer jobs can run the entire spectrum from working on a garbage truck or cleaning cesspools to serving as an engineering aide on a top-level scientific project—or traveling with a major league baseball club. Your age, experience, and training will determine the type of job you best fit into. Let us look at the various possibilities.

Stores, Wholesale and Retail

Warehouse work	Messenger
Sales clerk	Driver
Stock work	Maintenance/Custodian

71

Office Positions

Typist	Keypunch operator
Mail clerk	Office machine operator
File clerk	Telephone operator
Accountant	Bank clerk
Secretary	Receptionist
Duplicating clerk	Word processor

Office positions are one of the most common summer job groups for girls. Many organizations employ summer help to aid with vacation replacements, to provide a training ground for future employment prospects, or to get over peak workloads when the summer season is the busiest time of their year. As with all summer jobs, employment at a particular place—when you achieve a satisfactory work record—can almost assure you a job for future summers. Perhaps you can find permanent placement there when you are ready to work full-time.

Factories and Manufacturing Firms

Assembly	Packing
Machine operation	Shipping/Receiving
Maintenance/Custodial	Driving

Here again is the problem of summer replacements for vacations or simply a good practice of getting good future employees. However, many organizations that have seasonal work or holiday season work may find that the summertime is their season for preparing the product.

For example, many firms that manufacture items for Christmas must prepare during the summer months in order to fulfill orders when they arrive—such firms as toy makers, candy manufacturers, canneries, Christmas cards, and similar industries that depend upon this season: radio and television manufacturers, clothing makers, etc.

There are hundreds of such firms. When job hunting, determine what product is manufactured, when it is made, and when it is put on the market.

Construction Work

Laborers	Bricklayers
Drivers	Hod carriers
Surveyors	Painters
Trade helpers	Roofers
Carpenters	Masons

For males, this is one of the most popular summer jobs—as are clerical and restaurant jobs for girls. Here again, we have a prime season when the most work can and must be accomplished within a given period. Eligible youths can be in demand for these occupations. The work is hard, the hours are long (usually on an overtime basis), and the pay is among the highest in the various types of summer job.

Here you will need a different approach in acquiring work. Keep your eyes open for construction projects just being started or about to be started: roads, motels, hotels, schools, office buildings, railroads.

You may apply directly to the project superintendent, but you will usually be referred to a central office or a union hiring hall. In such instances, you must be prepared to join the union. The initiation fee and dues may eat into your first summer's earnings, but the union card may help you to get a job the following summer as well.

It would be wise to have a driver's license, also, and to learn to drive a vehicle with a manual gearshift. I have seen jobs lost because of the simple fact that an individual could handle only vehicles with automatic transmission.

Construction work is no picnic; there is a sacrifice for the good pay and premium hours, namely, hard physical labor. The first few days of hard labor—such as ditch digging, spreading cement, laying railroad ties, hod carrying—can be experiences you will never forget. However, the soreness will wear off in a few days. Stick with it! You may be tempted to leave the job, but do not be a quitter. Your reputation may follow you!

Hotels—Motels—Retaurants—Resorts

Here is a field that provides abundant jobs. This is seasonal, and

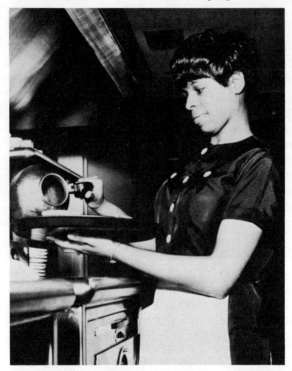

COURTESY OPPORTUNITIES INDUSTRIALIZATION CENTER, INC.
PHILADELPHIA, PENNSYLVANIA

*Food service operations offer many summer and part-
time job opportunities for teenagers.*

the time cycle coincides with the time that students are free to work.
The wide variety of jobs includes:

Waiters/Waitresses	Recreation specialists
Housekeepers	Life guards
Bussing	Babysitters
Golf caddies	Receptionists
Elevator operators	Telephone operators
Groundskeepers	Reservation clerks
Stable hands	Laundry workers
Maintenance workers	Ushers
Custodians	Bellhops
Office help	

Some of these jobs can be made even more interesting in that your meals and lodging may be provided. This is quite a saving if you must live away from home. Also, do not forget the tips or gratuities realized from some of these jobs. In such jobs you will usually meet many friendly people. Lifelong friendships and future contacts may be derived from this type of business and career opportunity.

Information on job possibilities and career information in this field may be obtained from:

American Hotel & Motel Association
22 West 57th Street
New York, N.Y. 10019

Farmwork

Although jobs are available in this field, they are becoming less prevalent because of many new sophisticated uses of farm machinery and other forms of mechanization. However, machine-operating jobs are still to be had, as well as such manual work as loading and unloading vehicles, cleaning stables and barns, maintenance work (fence building and mending, laying of wire, road repair, land clearance). Truck driving and hauling jobs are available and such other tasks as plant and fruit spraying, fruit and vegetable picking, greenhouse and nursery work, hay and straw baling, and, sometimes, sheep shearing.

Federal Agencies

A variety of positions is offered here, ranging from typists to scientific aides to clerk-carrier jobs in the Post Office Department to Forest Rangers.

Most teenagers would fall within the category of jobs in the GS1-X levels and PFS-5 (Post Office clerk-carrier) and are hired from a list of eligibles resulting from the Summer Employment Examinations.

The following information from a U.S. Civil Service Commission pamphlet describes the various work areas and ratings.

The number of jobs available is relatively small, and your chances of appointment depend upon the number and kind of summer jobs in the area where you apply, the number of applicants in that area, and your qualifications. Many more applicants than positions are available, so you would be wise not to apply for summer work solely with the federal government.

For the past several years, 25,000 jobs were filled from a list of nearly 6 times that many eligible applicants. More than three-fourths were typist and stenographer jobs, engineering and science-aide jobs, and clerk-carrier jobs with the Post Office Department.

Also limited oportunities existed for such jobs as clerks, office machine operators, library assistants, and medical and editorial assistants. Most jobs were in large metropolitan areas. In some parts of the country there were few or no opportunities in some occupations.

Clerk-carriers with the Post Office Department are employed for temporary work during the summer and may be considered for work during the Christmas season. Employment may be part-time in some cases. The work involves arduous duties such as unloading mailbags from trucks.

Eligibility is based on the written test. No education or experience is required. Most Post Office jobs require applicants to drive motor vehicles. For these jobs, applicants must be 18 years old and pass a driving performance test. Because of the high number of applicants, only competitors with scores in the 90 to 100 range receive consideration in most post offices.

All other jobs in this group are in grades GS-1 through 4. The following table gives a general relationship between the grade and the education or length of appropriate experience required.

Annual Pay Rates *(September 1981)*		*Education or* *Experience*
Grade 1	$7,960	No education or experience required
Grade 2	$8,951	High school or six months' experience
Grade 3	$9,766	One year's college or one year's experience
Grade 4	$10,963	Two years' college or two years' experience

Who May Apply for Jobs in This Group (Group I)

Any U.S. citizen may apply. The minimum age requirement is 18 at time of appointment to a summer job. However, this requirement is waived for high-school graduates who are at least 16 at the time of appointment.

Summer Employment Examination

This examination provides an opportunity for you to compete on a merit basis for a summer job. The examination will last 1½ hours and will measure vocabulary, reading comprehension, abstract reasoning, and table and chart interpretation.

SPECIAL PROVISION FOR THE WASHINGTON, D.C., METROPOLITAN AREA

In order to give wider geographic distribution to appointments in the nation's capital, first consideration for employment in GS-1 through FS-4 jobs in the Washington, D.C., metropolitan area is given to applicants whose legal residence is other than the District of Columbia, Maryland, or Virginia. Applicants for jobs in the Washington, D.C., metropolitan area who received scores of 95 or above and whose legal residence is outside those three areas will receive first consideration.

After those outside the area have been offered positions, then those applicants from the District of Columbia, Maryland, and Virginia who are in the same score range will be considered. This process is repeated in each score range. Your legal residence is your permanent residence, not the location of a school you may be attending temporarily.

Requirements for Typist and Stenographer Applicants

Some jobs—typist, stenographer, and certain machine operator positions requiring the use of a typewriter keyboard—need appropriate skills. If you want consideration for one of those jobs, you will be asked to furnish proof of proficiency when you are considered for a summer job. It will be to your advantage to obtain this proof as soon as possible. Any of the following is acceptable as evidence of your skills:

- A notice of rating from a typist or stenographer examination administered by (a) State or local Employment Service office or (b) a U.S. Civil Service Commission office.
- A certificate of proficiency dated within the last twelve months from your typing or shorthand teacher in (a) a public, parochial, or properly accredited private high school, or (b) a business, commercial, or secretarial school, or (c) a college or junior college, or (d) a school approved by the Veterans Administration for the education of veterans and their dependents.
- A certificate of proficiency dated within the last twelve months from a Job Corps center, a Neighborhood Youth Corps program, or a public or private social or welfare agency conducting programs sponsored or approved by the U.S. Office of Education, or by an appropriate State Office of Education.

A certificate of proficiency must indicate the number of words typed and/or recorded, the number of errors, and the length (time) of the test.

How to Apply

To apply for the written test required for jobs in Group I, you may file for an application, which may be obtained from college placement offices, most post offices, Interagency Boards of Examiners, and the U.S. Civil Service Examination.

Mail your application to:

> Summer Employment Examination
> U.S. Civil Service Commission
> 1900 E Street, N.W.
> Washington, D.C. 20415

Be sure to indicate on your application:

(1) The title of the examination: "Summer Employment Examination."

(2) The number of the announcement.

(3) The city, state, and test point number where you wish to take the written examination.

You will receive sample test questions and a notice of the time and place to report for the examination approximately five days be-

Teenagers perform a variety of duties when working at summer jobs and other temporary positions.

fore the scheduled test date. A listing of test dates and application deadlines is available at the same source from which you obtain the application.

Other positions are available within the federal government, but teenagers will have to have some college training in order to qualify. Among them are jobs in:

Department of Agriculture
    The Forest Service (forestry and related services—range management, landscape architecture).
Department of the Interior
    National Park Service (student assistant, landscape architect; student assistant, architect/history).

Bureau of Land Management (fire control aide, lookout, forestry and range aide, resources conservation, and recreation aide).
Department of State
Typists and stenographers, Washington, D.C., area.
Veterans Administration
Clerical occupations at regional offices, VA hospitals.

Summer Camp Work

This is an area in which the young teenager can begin his work experience and at the same time gain valuable knowledge about himself and experience for future jobs.

Camp work is a good source for the teenager's first job, since most factory jobs, construction work, and similar occupations have minimum age restrictions. The pay is not as inviting as it will be on future jobs, but the young person has little to offer in the way of experience or training. It must be considered, too, that in most cases room and board are included in the package. The work is outdoors, deals with young people, and is not as physically demanding as manual work.

For those young people who are planning careers with the retarded or handicapped, summer camp work can furnish true experience for the future, as many camps and local summer programs are dedicated to the care and therapy of such children.

Typical Jobs at Summer Camps

General camp counselor	Dramatics
Riding instructor	Canoeing/Boating
Water skiing	Hiking
Lifeguard	Photography
Arts and Crafts	Dancing
Nature study	Kitchen work
Athletics	Waiters
Art/Music/Ceramics	Laundry
Transportation operators	Groundskeeper
Nurses	Maintenance
Sailing	Waterfront maintenance

In looking over this list, you may have contributory experience despite the fact that you have not worked before. You may have had training with a musical instrument, athletics, art, sewing, cooking, Scouting, have taught Sunday school. Do not sell yourself short on these experiences.

COURTESY WASHINGTON CROSSING DAY CAMP
WASHINGTON CROSSING, PENNSYLVANIA

The summer camp offers many entry positions for teenagers.

Summer camps begin advertising for campers soon after Christmas. Ads can be found in the back of the magazine section of any large city newspaper. *The New York Times* has an especially fine advertising section on camps in the back part of its weekly magazine. The camps begin to advertise early in January, and that would not be too early for you to begin writing letters of application if you are interested in this type of summer employment.

SPECIAL SUMMER JOBS

Special or unique summer jobs worth pursuing that may or may not require experience are to be found in:

Country Clubs
Caddies	Table Waiting
Greens maintenance	Driving positions
Kitchen help	Bussing

Summer Stock Theaters
Bit-part acting
Chorus for singing and dancing (especially in music circus)
Wardrobe assistant
Usher
Doorkeeper
Parking lot attendant
Ticket office

Amusement Parks
Ticket taker
Ride operator
Refreshment stand attendant
Parking lot attendant
Maintenance

Then there are:

Moving companies, for those with muscles.
Gas station attendant.
Car washer.
Babysitter, for those who love children.
Tutor, for the person interested in teaching and learning teaching skills.
House painter.
Window washer.
Lawn maintenance, for the enterprising youth who can get out early enough in the spring to convince his neighbors they need him.

Ice cream routes—a job that can be run by two girls as well as two boys.

Hospital aides—for those youths who want to find out how deep their interest in nursing really is.

Attendants at baseball games or other sporting events.

Playgrounds—a job almost equal to being counselor at a day camp, for those who want to work or learn to work with children.

Do not forget the money-makers that are sometimes hardly considered jobs by regular standards. I recall the young boy (now a college graduate and a successful guidance counselor) who cultivated fishing worms in his backyard. He was fortunate in living on a street that was a direct route to a favorite fishing area. By selling his night crawlers to anxious anglers, he was able to pay the greater part of his college expenses.

WHERE AND HOW TO APPLY

When to apply for the summer job is important, again, because of the short time span within which you must operate. You should begin the job hunt between Christmas and Easter and no later than April 1. Many of the seasonal businesses must have their manpower programs set early. This is an important phase of the business. Golf courses, seashore resort, and summer camps are a few examples. Some of them may even begin hiring during weekends even before is out.

In fact, applications for jobs in many federal agencies must be postmarked no later than January 30 of the year in which you are applying for the job. You must meet this deadline in order to be eligible to take the written tests for the lower-level positions. In reality, they encourage applicants to begin applying for those jobs in mid-October of the year preceding the one in which they want to work.

You can apply in person or by letter in order to "get your foot in the door"—utilizing techniques described earlier regarding résumés, letters, the interview, and other important points.

It is wise to use Christmas vacation, Easter holidays, and midyear breaks for job hunting. You may even be able to acquire a part-time job during those free times that could automatically lead to a summer position.

Where can you get leads about jobs? Who can give you the information? Try these sources:

School counselors
Teachers (who teach in the area of your Interest)
Friends and neighbors
State Employment Service
Private employment agencies
School bulletin boards
Newspaper ads
Run an ad yourself in the "Situations Wanted" section
Store windows
Ads on supermarket bulletin boards
Chambers of Commerce
Direct application
Youth Employment Service
Milkmen, postmen, and person with similar jobs who come into
    contact with many, many people

As of this writing, the federal government has set aside funds for teenagers who come from families that are financially deprived. There is a variety of jobs—summer positions, work while attending school, etc. Check with your local state employment service.

Age Restriction

Your age will be a prime factor in determining the type of job you should seek—and may be able to obtain. Here are some basic guidelines on what you can expect. These are the types of job suitable—and permissible—under the Fair Labor Standards Act. They are also further regulated by various state bureaus on wages and hours.

Since many high-school students will need working papers, most school guidance counselors are familiar with the hours of work permitted and the limitations on the types of job you can seek.

The following information from a New Jersey State Employment Service bulletin can be of some help:

Jobs for Boys 14 to 15 Years of Age

Delivery on foot or bicycle (not motorized) for grocery stores, markets, cleaners, tailors, newspapers, etc.

Salesclerks, stock boys, wrappers and packers in retail stores and offices.

Chore boys and mowers of lawns (if not power machine).

Caddies, attendants at places of amusement, pin setters in public or private bowling alleys.

Farm and nursery laborers.

Restaurant and soda fountain workers—except where alcoholic beverages are sold—and except as carhops.

Jobs for Girls 14 to 15 Years of Age

Sales personnel, stock people, wrappers, packers, clerical workers in retail stores.

Domestic service workers, mother's helpers, babysitters in private homes and day nurseries.

Clerical workers in stores, offices.

Nurses' aides.

Restaurant and soda fountain workers—except where alcoholic beverages are sold—and except as carhops.

Attendants at places of amusement.

Farm laborers (picking vegetable and fruit crops primarily).

Jobs for Boys 16 and 17 Years of Age

Sales personnel, stock boys, wrappers, packers, and delivery boys in retail and wholesale establishments.

Helpers to mechanics and other skilled craftsmen—if not in the construction industry.

Restaurant and soda fountain employees, carhops, except where alcoholic beverages are sold.

Delivery messenger—except as drivers or helpers on motor vehicles if the employer is in interstate commerce.

Factory operators.

Clerical and office workers.

Counselors and assistants at recreation centers and camps.

Laboratory assistants—except with hazardous materials.
Laundry workers.

Jobs for Girls 16 and 17 Years of Age

Salespeople, merchandise helpers, wrappers, and packers in wholesale and retail establishments.
Clerical and office workers.
Restaurant and soda fountain employees, carhops, except where alcoholic beverages are sold.
Telephone and telegraph operators.
Beauty parlor operators and helpers.
Factory workers except in the production of goods for the U.S. Government under the Walsh-Healey Public Contracts Act.
Nurses' aides and laboratory assistants, except with hazardous substances.
Laundry workers.
Counselors and assistants at camps and recreation centers.

Part-Time Jobs

Part-time jobs are a way of life today with students, wives, mothers holding down part-time jobs. Even full-time workers have multiple jobs or do "moonlighting." The primary motivation appears to be the familiar story: a search for increased income.

According to the Bureau of Labor Statistics, moonlighting habits of the American worker have increased drastically.

Why do people hold these extra jobs? For the simple reason that they wish to live at a higher standard and be able to buy more things. Further, the present high cost of living necessitates more income. Isn't this true for the teenager? He wants to be independent—to earn money so he can buy the things he ordinarily could not afford, to update his wardrobe, buy a car, have more money for dates, movies, hamburgers.

Our economy today lends itself to an availability of part-time jobs. Rather than hire full-time workers, employers will take up the slack with "part-timers," "casuals," "moonlighters," "temporaries"—call them what you will. Also, with a shorter work week (thirty-five to forty hours) and longer vacations, workers have more leisure time, and some people prefer to work rather than just "vacation." These include such people as teachers, policemen, firemen, postal workers, farmers, and similar occupations. (A farmer can moonlight by driving a school bus, for example, and still have time to run his farm in his "off season.")

A trend in the 80's is job-sharing and flextime where a full-time job is shared, usually by husband and wife, for example a teaching post at a college. This releases both for research, family shared re-

COURTESY CREATIVE PLAYTHINGS, INC.
PRINCETON, NEW JERSEY

Sales occupations provide many part-time and temporary positions for teenagers.

sponsibilities or other activities. Flextime offers such alternatives as a 10 hour day with 4 day week as opposed to the 8 hour day and 5 day week.

The increasing rate of part-time workers is partly the result of middle-aged women coming into the labor force. Most of the increase was among these women entering or returning to the labor force after their children enter school, whereas others wait until later when college expenses for their children or other needs require additional income.

In a recent fifteen-year period the number of part-time women workers rose by 70 percent, double the percentage increase among full-time workers.

Among men, the contrast was even more striking. The number of part-time workers rose by 53 percent, five times the increase among full-time workers. *Most of this sharp rise was because of the increasing numbers of youths who entered the work force to take part-time work while attending school. The number of teenage boys working part-time more than doubled.*

The proportion of women with work experience rose from 41 to 48 percent, whereas there was a decline of men with work experience. This decline was almost entirely the result of increased retirement, as older men found it easier to retire because of expanded coverage and increased benefits under Social Security and company retirement and pension plans.

In the last fifteen years a noticeable rise has taken place in the number of women entering or reentering the labor force. Women have combined the paycheck with the apron, stimulating the growth of companies producing frozen dinners.

It is the older women, 45 to 64 years of age, who have shown the greatest tendency to start or return to work.

It is becoming less common for women to leave the labor force permanently at the time of marriage or first pregnancy. Women, especially the better educated, now often spend a few years outside before entering or reentering the labor force. Also, the heavy demand for workers and the greater opportunities for part-time work have led many companies actively to seek out women workers. The 1964 Civil Rights Act has opened up many occupations previously closed to them. Employment opportunities for women are expanding greatly, and the outlook for the future is for more of the same.

The proportion of single girls working has trended downward during these fifteen years while the proportion of married women has gone up. This has resulted from the increasing tendency of older married women to enter the labor force while the greater proportion of young girls, most of whom are single, stay in school longer.

The proportion of white women working over these years has trended steadily upward, while that of Negro women has fallen slightly. It can be expected that this trend will continue as American society and standards become more homogeneous.

From the same report we find figures regarding the number of youths holding part-time jobs. Of the number of persons from 14 to 17 years of age with some type of previous work experience, almost

50 percent worked at part-time jobs. In the 18- to 19-year-old group almost 75 percent worked part-time. So you see, it *is* fashionable to take part-time jobs, and it *is* a fact of life. The definition of a part-time worker is one who has worked less than thirty-five hours per week during a period of 6½ weeks or more.

In what types of industry do most of the people work? Virtually all types of organizations are represented, but the largest numbers are in the following areas:

Printing, publishing, newspapers, and allied groups
Wholesale and retail organizations
Entertainment and recreational services
Educational services
Private households (maids, cleaning women, babysitters, gardeners)
Food products
Forestry and fisheries
Medical and health services
Transportation services
Farm work

Where Are the Part-Time Jobs?

As was said earlier, many part-time jobs can be acquired at the same sources as those for summer positions. However, summer jobs are seasonal, and if you want a part-time job for the whole year (a full-time part-time job!), you will have to become resourceful and make a more extensive search.

Where to Go?

Just as summer jobs are held for a certain period of the year, part-time jobs are held for a given time during the day and/or week. In reviewing the list below, you will notice that the organizations lend themselves to part-time hours:

Stores: evening hours or weekends. Buying habits have changed (to a large degree because so many more women are working during the day and cannot shop), and most sales outlets are open during the evening and weekends.

Factories: partial shifts of four to six hours are sometimes established when there is a lack of full-time workers. The same is true of weekends. Some manufacturing plants will provide transportation if there is a scarcity of labor in the immediate population area. Many firms rely upon college students for a source of labor.

COURTESY HOTEL HERSHEY
HERSHEY, PENNSYLVANIA

Hotels and resort areas such as the Hotel Hershey offer summer job opportunities to young people.

Restaurants: peak hours are naturally mealtimes, and usually from lunch through the dinner hour.

Hotels-Motels: mealtimes, check in/out times, or evenings are prime times (banquets, meetings, etc.).

Private Homes: the familiar gardening and landscaping jobs, babysitting, window washing, cleaning.

Offices: afternoon, evening, or Saturday work when full-time workers are not warranted, or work on a given day must be prepared for the next morning or over the weekend. This is a good spot for typists, secretaries, keypunchers, and other clerical workers.

Special Areas:
Parking lot attendant

Ushers, ticket takers, or concessionnaires attendant at sporting events

Car washer

Caddying on weekends until school is out

Greenhouse work

Federally sponsored projects: Neighborhood Youth Corps, Youth Opportunity Center (YOC)

Schools: teacher aides, groundskeepers, janitorial service

Direct sales: magazines, newspapers, kitchenware, books, cosmetics, brushes

Typing and thesis typing

Business route: pizza sales, dry cleaning, etc.

Telephone operator: night answering service or telephone sales clerk

Do not forget the peak holiday seasons, especially Christmas. Look at these possibilities:

Postal jobs	Department stores
Florists	Toy shops
Candy stores	Mail-order houses
Store dealing solely in holiday products at Christmas	

Organizations exist that specialize in placing people into part-time or temporary positions. In the secretarial/clerical areas the most famous is the Kelly Services or "Kelly Girl." Kelly Girl has three hundred branch offices in the United States and Canada. No fee is charged for job placement.

Other similar organizations may be found in the Yellow Pages of the telephone directory under "Temporary Employment Contractors." In addition to Kelly Services, there are Manpower, Inc., Western Girl, Employers Overload, Olsten Services, and others.

CHAPTER VI

The Armed Forces

As high-school graduation draws near, the armed forces may occupy a prominent place in the minds of most teenagers. Many teenagers will possibly consider a career in a branch of the armed forces or seek to be appointed as a cadet at one of the service academies. Girls are not excluded from making careers in the armed forces. Many will seek careers of responsibility with one of the services or academies.

We cannot take the time to describe all the branches of the service in great detail, but we will give a review of screening procedures, types of test, occupational fields, areas of training, academy entrance requirements, and related areas.

Counseling Information

The armed forces work closely with high-school counselors and other school officials, since the student body is a prime source of potential enlistees. The following information derived from Department of Defense literature for high school counselors provides useful information about this cooperative effort.

Most of the high schools in the country will be approached by recruiting personnel interested in arranging for the administration of the Armed Services Vocational Aptitude Battery (ASVAB) to high-school seniors. The military services use this test battery to stimulate interest in military careers and to provide young persons, high-school counselors, and the individual services with information on vocational aptitudes of high-school seniors as indicated by their test scores.

To put a minimum load on already crowded high-school schedules, the military services have developed in the ASVAB a single test battery for all the services. In the past, several of the services approached the high schools with their own tests. Use of this single battery simplifies school-military relationships, and provides test scores for use in career counseling for all the military services.

The test battery requires about 2½ hours for administration, The tests are sent to a central facility for scoring. Counselors and the military recruiters are provided with scores for the students who took the test, about thirty days after administration. Counselors will pro-

COURTESY U.S. ARMY

The Cadet Corps at the U.S. Military Academy passes in review.

vide the test scores to the students and discuss the meaning of the results with them.

Aptitude scores are not the sole criterion of acceptability for military service. An individual's acceptance for enlistment and his ultimate duty assignment are determined by the individual service based on the needs of the service in relation to his aptitude.

The Armed Services
Vocational Aptitude Battery

Psychologists have long realized that various occupations require varying aptitudes. For that reason, tests that measure specific aptitudes may predict success or failure with more accuracy than general intelligence or overall ability tests. The ASVAB was developed with this concept in mind. The young men and women tested, as well as the military services, benefit from the improved job placement possible with measurement of specific aptitudes.

The component tests in the ASVAB are given below. Specific aptitude area scores are calculated using combinations of the scores on these component tests.

Tests in the ASVAB

The twelve tests in the ASVAB are basically paper-and-pencil tests. Below are short descriptions of the tests.

(1) *General Information.* This test will consist of fifteen general information questions concerning a variety of topics. Topics include questions on geography, sports, literature, history, and other areas. Each question is followed by four possible answers from which you are to select the correct response.

(2) *Numerical Operations.* This test will contain fifty mathematical computations, each followed by four possible answers. You are to rapidly determine which of the four answers is correct.

(3) *Attention to Detail.* This test will contain thirty items designed to measure speed and accuracy. Each item contains the letters O and C. There will be at least 11 and not more than 15 C's in each item. You are to count the number of C's in each.

(4) *Word Knowledge.* This test is designed to measure your understanding of the meaning of words. The test will consist of thirty underlined words, each followed by four alternate words. From the four choices, you are to select the word meaning most nearly the same as the underlined word.

(5) *Arithmetic Reasoning.* This test will consist of twenty arithmetic reasoning problems. In each case, you are to solve the problem and then select the correct answer from four alternatives.

(6) *Space Perception Test.* This test will contain twenty pictorial items. Each shows a flat pattern followed by four drawings of three dimensional figures. You are to select the three dimesional figure which could be made from the pattern by folding it on the dotted lines.

(7) *Mathematics Knowledge.* This test will contain twenty questions designed to measure general mathematical knowledge. Included are questions on algebra and geometry. Each question is followed by four possible answers from which you are to select the correct response.

(8) *Electronics Information.* This test will consist of thirty questions dealing with electricity, radio principles, and electronics. Each question is followed by four possible answers, from which you are to select the best response.

(9) *Mechanical Comprehension.* This test will contain twenty questions designed to measure your understanding of mechanical principles. Many of the questions use drawings to illustrate specific principles. Each question is followed by four possible answers from which you are to select the correct response.

(10) *General Science.* This test will consist of twenty questions encompassing both physical and biological sciences. Each question is followed by four alternatives from which you are to select the correct answer.

(11) *Shop Information.* This test will consist of twenty questions about shop procedures and the use of tools. Each question is followed by four alternatives from which you are to select the correct answer.

(12) *Automotive Information.* This test will contain twenty questions designed to measure your knowledge of how automobiles function. Some of the questions concerning automotive repair and parts are rather technical in nature, while others require a general understanding and recognition of various malfunctions. Each question is followed by four alternatives from which you are to select the best response.

Below is a list of typical occupational fields that are listed by aptitude area:

Electronics Aptitude Area:
   Missile and fire-control electronic maintenance
   Data-processing equipment maintenance
   Wire maintenance
   Communications electronic maintenance
   Armament systems maintenance

General Mechanical Aptitude Area:
  Precision instruments and gauges maintenance
  Metalworking
  Building construction trades
  Munitions and weapons maintenance
  Industrial gas production
  Liquid fuel system maintenance
  Office machine maintenance
  Boiler operation and maintenance
  Electric power generation and distribution
  Fire protection
  Freight operations
  Fueling operations
  Optical maintenance
  Deep-sea diving
  Blasting operations
  Patternmaking
  Shipfitting
  Aviation structural mechanics
  Air conditioning and refrigeration
  Molding
  Shipboard machinery operation and maintenance
  Machinist's operations

Motor Mechanical Aptitude Area:
  Heavy construction equipment operation and maintenance
  Automotive operation and maintenance
  Aircraft maintenance
  Diesel engine maintenance
  Gas turbine engine operation and maintenance
  Aviation support equipment, operation, and maintenance
  Railway equipment maintenance
  Railway operations

Clerical Administrative Aptitude Area:
  Clerical administration
  Communications operations
  Accounting and finance
  Data processing

Supply services
Procurement services
Statistical services
Chaplain services
Personnel services
Transportation services
Recreation services

General Technical Aptitude Area:
Drafting, illustrating, and mapping
Surveying
Printing
Photography
Medical and dental services
Food service
Law enforcement
Intelligence
Weather service
Information service
Air traffic control and warning
Aircraft and shipboard communications and navigation
Military bands

Your first exposure to the military screening process will either be at your high school or at the local recruiting station.

This prescreening will simply involve the competion of a single employment application and usually an Enlistment Screening Test before you go to another center—usually a larger city—for further screening or an Applicant Qualifying Test (AQT).

You can expect the following basic requirements for admission; they will vary with enlistment demands (1978).

> *Age:* The normal entry age is 18, but with parental consent it can be 17.
> *Education:* High-school graduate preferred.
> *Citizenship:* You must be a citizen or have declared your intent to become a citizen.
> *Physical condition:* Must pass a physical, but normal health will usually insure this.

Character: Must have good character with average or above-average learning ability. Must pass a written test.
Marital status: Single or married.
Term: Two to six years depending upon the branch of service.

If you have not taken the tests as described above, you can expect them at this larger center. In the case of the Army, this is the Armed Forces Examination and Entrance Station. Here you will receive another physical exam and the Oath of Enlistment. You are then officially in the Army.

After that comes the Reception Center, where you receive uniform clothing, personal equipment, and are inoculated against certain diseases. Test scores are carefully studied and these, coupled with an intensive interview, play a great part in your first job classification.

It is not in the interest of this book to describe full pay allowances, other dollar benefits, promotion, and educational opportunities. Space does not permit such details.

Equal opportunity exists in all branches of the armed forces for women and minority groups. No special privileges are accorded any groups, as they are all subject to the same regulations and rights as all other servicemen.

The Service Academies

To describe the entrance requirements of all the service academies would take a book in itself. Therefore, I shall attempt to give some insight into what can be expected, with the hope that this will instill enough interest for the teenager to pursue the matter further.

We will outline the general requirements for the U.S. Air Force Academy, eight miles north of Colorado Springs, Colorado.

The following information was taken from the Air Force Academy pamphlet "Admissions Information for High School Counselors."

ADMISSION REQUIREMENTS

Nomination

The Academy's admissions procedures differ from those of civilian institutions primarily because an official nomination is required. A

The eagle statue in foreground symbolizes the mission
of the Air Force Academy. Cadets come to the Academy
to gain academic and military skills that will fit them
for a career of service to their country. In the back-
ground are the multispired all-faith chapel and the Front
Range of the Rocky Mountains.

majority of the nominations are allotted to members of Congress. No political affiliation is necessary to apply to a congressman for a nomination. U.S. Senators and Representatives want to receive applications from young people who will have a chance to qualify for the Academy. Applications must be sent directly to the Congressmen. You may submit requests to more than one member. You may apply to the U.S. Representative of your congressional district as well as to the two U.S. Senators of your state.

Each congressman may determine his own nomination procedure, and since many rely on testing to screen their applicants, the request for nomination should be submitted as early as the *spring of the applicant's junior year in high school.* Some people fail to be considered for admission immediately after high-school graduation because they do not apply soon enough. An individual must obtain a nomination in time to take the entrance examinations given from November through March, preceding admission of the cadet class in June.

The following is a breakdown of the various sources of nomination. Appointment by U.S. Senators and Representatives accounts for a major portion of those selected. Cumulative appointments are the total number available, of which about one-fourth enter every year. The other opportunities are filled annually.

Source of Nomination	*Authorized Appointments* (*Cumulative*)
U.S. Senators (5 each)	500
U.S. Representatives (5 each)	2,175
Vice President	5
District of Columbia	5
Puerto Rico	6
Canal Zone	1
American Samoa, Guam, Virgin Islands	1
Sons of deceased or disabled veterans	40
Allied Students	
Republic of the Philippines	4
American Republics	20
	(*Annual*)
Presidential	100
Regular components	85
Honor military and naval schools	
AFROTC and AF Jr. ROTC	20
Qualified alternates	150
Sons of Medal of Honor winners	No limit

Applications should be submitted to the proper category if nomination by a Senator or Congressman is not sought.

Members of Congress may request information from high-school principals or counselors to assist in making an evaluation of an applicant's potential. Congressional members may ask for school transcripts as well as the numerical rank of a student in his class.

An applicant must be 17 years of age and not have passed his or her 22nd birthday on July 1 of the year of admission. He or she must be a citizen of the United States, but allied students are exempt from graduation. Applicants must be unmarried.

Academics

One of the best indicators of an applicant's success at the Academy is his academic standing in his high-school class. A candidate is not likely to receive an appointment unless he ranks in the upper 40 percent. It is possible for a student who does not rank in the upper 40 percent of his class to compensate by attending a preparatory school or college for a year to improve his performance.

Most Congressmen require their applicants to take the Civil Service Designation Examination as a preliminary screening exam. A score of 70 or better indicates that the young person has a chance to make it on the College Entrance Examination Board test, which is the required exam for Academy entrance. Particulars of this exam can be obtained from the guidance counselor in your school.

Leadership

Since the Academy prepares cadets to become leaders in the Air Force, qualities of leadership are important elements in the selection of candidates for appointment. Probably the best indicator of leadership potential is the degree of an applicant's participation and distinction in extracurricular high-school activities, such as being elected class president or earning an athletic award, rather than joining in a variety of activities without evidence of leadership.

Physical

Students preparing for the Academy should maintain a high degree of physical fitness through participation in sports and proper health care. There is a definite correlation between physical fitness and the ability to succeed in the Academy program.

A Physical Aptitude Examination is given to each candidate to measure coordination, strength, endurance, and agility. Candidates may prepare for this exam by engaging regularly in vigorous physical activity such as running, exercises, and sports. A cadet's first two months at the Academy are devoted to a strenuous physical program of basic cadet training. Physical exertion is required from morning until night as the cadet goes through physical conditioning and military training. A basic cadet must be conditioned to meet the stringent physical demands that will be placed upon him.

COURTESY U.S. AIR FORCE ACADEMY, COLORADO

Air Force Academy Cadets vie for top honors during annual Field Day. This activity is typical of the physical conditioning Cadets receive as they prepare for their future roles as Air Force leaders.

Motivation

An applicant's purpose in seeking a nomination is important. Students who are considering the Academy should be sure that they are willing to lead a disciplined pattern of life as cadets and that they are prepared for the total involvement necessary to accomplish the Academy program. A person should not apply primarily to please others or to gain a free education. Experience has proved that those reasons do not provide sufficient motivation for a cadet to succeed through four years that require considerable self-discipline and application of effort.

The armed forces or the service academies are interesting careers. If a longtime career is contemplated, many benefits from your training can be applied in civilian life after retirement. Most Army retirements occur after twenty years of service, which places the retiree in the early 40's. This is well below the age at which a person would be retired from a civilian occupation, so an applicant can really look ahead to having two careers in one lifetime.

On a short-range basis, you can experience excellent training for civilian jobs. The technical training received in the armed forces is the best in the country. With travel and the maturity derived from the unique experiences of serving in the armed forces, you can come home ready to take up the rest of your life.

Women in the Armed Forces

In order to give "equal time" to the Navy, the feminine portion of this chapter will deal with information from the U.S. Navy and its career opportunities for women. Since high-school graduates will usually enter the armed forces as enlisted personnel, we shall talk about the Navy enlisted woman.

In the Navy, women serve in all 85 ratings except 5 which require considerable physical strength.

Women can serve in the following ratings and even more occupational categories:

Aerographer's mate	Electronics technician
Air control	Hospital corps
Aviation electronics technician	Illustrator-Drafting
Aviation maintenance adminis-	Journalist
tration	Personnel
Aviation storekeeper	Photographer's mate
Data-processing technician	Radio operator
Data systems technician	Storekeeper
Dental technician	Yeoman
Disbursing clerk	

Women enlisted in the regular Navy are assigned to naval activities in the United States. Later they may be transferred to another activity in the States or, when qualified, to overseas stations. The normal

A Navy recruiter explains training and career opportunities to prospective seaman.

tour of duty is eighteen to twenty-four months overseas and three years in the United States. Women are subject to the same regulations and advancement in rating as men. They have the same compensation, benefits, and privileges as men, and attend the same training schools for the ratings applicable.

The Navy is essentially a military organization and all personnel conform to rules and regulations to maintain an efficient shore establishment. All personnel must assume routine or non-related responsibilities to contribute to efficient operation of the Navy, including the military procedures for the care of uniforms, personal belongings, and living quarters.

Qualifications and Preparation

Any woman who meets the following standards is eligible for enlistment in the regular Navy:

Age: Applicants must be between the ages of 17 and 31 inclusive. Parental consent is required for applicants who are 17 years of age.

Citizenship: Must be a citizen of the United States, or an alien who has declared intent of becoming a U.S. citizen.

Physical: Must meet the physical standards prescribed by the Manual of the Medical Department for Enlisted Women. Applicants will be given the Armed Forces Women's Aptitude Selection Test.

Education: Applicants must have a high-school education or equivalent.

Character: Applicants must be of good character and must provide a list of references who can attest to this fact.

Term of Enlistment: Applicants enlist for three, four, or six years at their own option.

Training Provided

Upon entering the Navy, all women are sent to a Recruit Training Command for basic training, guidance, and classification. Upon completion of this period, further training may be obtained at Navy schools, through on-the-job training, and through the study of manuals provided for advancement in rating.

Health and Welfare

The Navy is concerned about the health and welfare of the women in its service. To insure the well-being of all, the Navy provides comfortable living quarters, good food, the best in medical and dental care, opportunity to participate in the religious service of one's choice, and recreational facilities for sports and leisure-time activities.

Enlistment Procedures

Enlistment is accomplished through U.S. Navy recruiting stations. Those interested should visit their nearest Navy recruiting station to learn about the opportunities for women and how women serve and live in the Navy.

To enlist in the Navy, men and women must be between 17 and 31 years of age. Parental or guardian consent is required for 17-year olds. They must be citizens or immigrant aliens with immigration and naturalization forms. A physical examination to prove normal health is also required. There are no specific educational requirements, but the Navy prefers high school graduates. Both single and married men and women are accepted.

CHAPTER VII

Nursing

When casual surveys of junior- and senior-high-school girls are made regarding occupations girls would like to pursue, the answer many of them will give will be nursing. Nursing, secretarial/clerical work, teaching, and sales are probably the most popular choices of the teenager.

This is borne out by the fact that in 1978, nearly 1,059,000 registered professional nurses (R.N.'s) were employed in the United States. In addition, replacement positions as well as growth positions will provide for an additional 500,000 or more nurses. Replacement and growth positions are about equally contained in this total.

Another interesting fact is that of all the professional occupations, nursing ranks third, the first two being teaching and scientific/technical areas. These data are from the U.S. Bureau of the Census and Bureau of Labor Statistics.

Although many women are in nursing, the road to becoming an R.N. is not an easy one. You need the education, patience, and a sincere interest in people, plus the desire to care for the sick and injured. You must be dependable, alert, possess good judgment, and be physically strong. Many people—and their lives—will depend upon you if you achieve your goal.

The "Occupational Outlook Handbook" provides the following information on training, qualifications, and opportunities for advancement in the nursing profession.

A license is required in order to practice professional nursing in all of the states and the District of Columbia. To be licensed, a nurse must have graduated from a school approved by a state board of nursing and pass a state board examination. A nurse may be licensed in more than one state, either by examination or by endorsement of a license issued by another state.

High-school graduation is required for admission to all schools of professional nursing. Many schools accept only graduates in the upper third or upper half of their class. Students are required to be competent in science and math, with emphasis on biology and chemistry with laboratory work.

Three types of educational program offer the basic education required for careers in professional nursing: the diploma, baccalaureate degree, and associate degree.

Diploma programs are conducted by hospital and independent schools and usually require three years of training. A bachelor-degree program usually requires four years of study in a college or university, although a few require five years. The associate-degree programs in junior and community colleges require approximately two years of nursing education.

In 1974, more than 1,400 programs of these three types were offered in the United States. Diploma programs accounted for about two-thirds of the total, the remainder being divided evenly between associate and baccalaureate-degree programs.

All programs include classroom instruction and supervised nursing practice. Students take courses in anatomy, physiology, microbiology, nutrition, psychology, and basic nursing care.

Students are given practical experience under close supervision in the care of patients with various types of illnesses. Programs are carried on in both hospitals and other health facilities. Students in colleges offering bachelor-degree programs are assigned to public health agencies, where they learn to care for patients in clinics and in the patients' homes. General education is combined with nursing education in baccalaureate- and associate-degree programs and in some diploma programs as well.

Hospital nursing usually begins with staff positions from which experienced nurses may be advanced to progressively more responsible supervisory positions such as head nurse, supervisor, assistant director, and ultimately, the director of nursing service.

A master's degree is often required for supervisory and administrative positions, as well as for positions in nursing education, clinical specialization, and research. In public health agencies, advancement opportunities are usually limited for nurses without degrees in public health nursing.

Hospital nurses are the largest group of registered nurses. Most of these are staff nurses who perform skilled bedside nursing such as

caring for a patient after an operation by assisting with blood trans-
fusions and intravenous feedings, and giving medications.

They also supervise auxiliary nursing workers. Some hospital
nurses work primarily in the operating room. Others limit their work
to certain types of patients, such as children, the elderly, or the
mentally ill. Still others are engaged primarily in administrative work.

Private-duty nurses give individual nursing care to patients who
need constant attention. In hospitals, one private-duty nurse may
sometimes take care of a few patients who require special nursing
care but not full-time attention.

Office nurses assist physicians and dental surgeons, and occasion-
ally dentists, in the care of patients in private practice or clinics.
Sometimes they perform routine laboratory and office work.

Public health nurses care for patients in clinics, or visit them in
their homes. Their duties include teaching patients and families about
basic nursing care for home-bound patients. They give periodic
nursing care to a home-bound patient as prescribed by a physician.
They demonstrate diet plans to groups of patients. They arrange for
immunization programs for the community or a special group. These
nurses work with community leaders, teachers, parents, and physicians in community health education programs. Some public-health
nurses work in schools.

School nurses have interesting positions in that they continually
deal with young people. These are choice positions, since the working
hours are short and not regular as is the case with the hospital or
office nurse. The vacations and holidays of the school systems are
the same for the nurse as for the students, which of course means a
long vacation at Christmas and an even longer one in the summertime. This is ideal for a nurse who is also a mother with school-age
children.

An even more attractive side of school nursing is that the degree
nurses usually receive salaries equal to those of teachers. Such
salaries far exceed most other types of nursing positions for a shorter
work year. Also, there is not shift work as in hospitals.

Nursing educators teach students the principles and skills of nursing both in the classroom and at the bedside. They may also conduct
refresher and in-service courses for registered nurses.

Occupational health or industrial nurses provide nursing care to employees working in industry and government, and, along with physicians, are responsible for promoting employee health. They may work alone (with a doctor on call), or they may be a part of a health service staff in a large organization. As directed by a doctor, they treat minor injuries and illnesses occurring at the place of employment, provide for any needed nursing care, arrange for further medical care if necessary, and offer health counseling. They may also assist with health examinations and inoculations to help prevent or control diseases.

Nurses also engage in activities such as research or serving on the staffs of nursing organizations.

As mentioned above, the employment outlook for nurses is most favorable. For those who have had graduate education, the outlook is excellent for obtaining positions as administrators, teachers, clinical specialists, public health nurses, and for work in research.

Among the principal factors underlying the anticipated rise in the demand for nurses are the improved economic status of the population; extension of prepayment programs for hospitalization and medical care, including Medicare and Medicaid; expansion of medical services as a result of new medical techniques and new drugs; and increased interest in preventive medicine and rehabilitation of the handicapped.

The anticipated rise in demand for registered nurses is expected to be accompanied by a rapid increase in the number of graduating nurses. This growth is expected to result from increasing numbers of high-school graduates who will enter nursing schools, and from the construction of additional nursing-school facilities. These facilities will be financed in part from funds provided by the Health Facilities Act and the Nurse Training Act.

Moreover, under the Nurse Training Act, a needy student may obtain a loan, a portion of which need not be repaid if the student obtains full-time employment in nursing after graduation. The Nurse Training Act also provides funds to cover tuition, fees, and a stipend and allowances for trainees seeking advanced training for positions as administrators, supervisors, nursing specialists, and nurse educators. In addition to the anticipated increase in the number of new graduates entering nursing each year, an increase is also expected in the number of inactive nurses who will return to work.

For those students who need financial help, various scholarships and federal aid are available.

The Bureau of Health Professions Education and Manpower Training administers the Nursing Student Loan Program and the Nursing Scholarship Program, which provide financial assistance to full-time students enrolled in schools participating in those programs. The purpose of the programs is to aid students who need assistance in pursuing a diploma in nursing, an associate degree, or a baccalaureate or graduate degree in nursing.

Any citizen or national of the United States enrolled in a school in the United States, Puerto Rico, the Canal Zone, Guam, American Samoa, or the Virgin Islands that participates in the programs is eligible to apply for a loan or scholarship.

A student or prospective student must obtain further information about financial assistance from the school where she intends to apply for admission or is enrolled.

The Office of Education, Department of Health, Education, and Welfare also administers several programs that provide students with financial aid. They include the National Defense Student Loan Program, the Guaranteed Loan Program, the Vocational Loan Program, and a Work-Study Program. Information on the programs may also be obtained from the school in which you are enrolled.

It is suggested that, at the time you apply for admission to a school or college, you discuss your financial needs with the admissions officer or the director of student financial aid of the school.

Nursing Careers in the Armed Forces

Nursing careers in the armed forces can be interesting because of the traveling involved and the great variety of duties. We shall not attempt to describe nursing in all the various branches of the armed forces. Instead, we will zero in on one branch of the service and look at the Navy nurse.

In order to qualify as a Navy nurse, you must be a registered nurse or a student in a diploma program or four-year college program. Student nurses enrolled in diploma nursing education programs of at least three academic years' duration may apply for an officer's commission in the Direct Appointment Program.

To qualify for the Navy Nurse Corps Candidate Program, you must be:

(1) Male or female junior or senior collegiate student enrolled in an accredited school.

(2) A U.S. citizen, regardless of race, creed, or nationality; or an

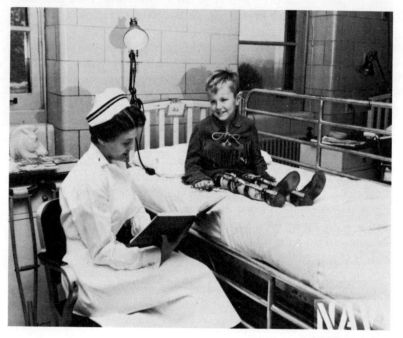

The Navy nurse has a variety of duties, as evidenced by this scene in a U.S. Naval Hospital orthopedic ward.

alien graduate nurse of an approved School of Nursing in the U.S., Canada, or Puerto Rico residing in the U.S. and who has declared intent for U.S. citizenship.

(3) Physically qualified according to Navy standards.

(4) Willing to serve three years of active duty.

(5) No marital restrictions.

Applicants enrolled in an accredited collegiate school of nursing may be eligible to enroll as a Navy Nurse Corps Candidate and complete her education *at Navy expense.*

The Navy attempts to assign you to a Naval hospital of your choice and also to the clinical specialty in which you are most interested:

General medicine	Orthopedics
General surgery	Ophthalmology
Plastic surgery	Otorhinolaryngology
Dental surgery	Pediatrics
Urology	Emergency room
Thoracic surgery	Operating room
Obstetrics and gynecology	Inservice education
Psychiatry	Outpatient clinics
Neurosurgery	Critical care units

The armed forces are advanced in scientific and technological techniques.

"Hyperbaric nursing" is a fairly recent in-service training program for Navy nurses. The first class was graduated in May, 1967, at New London, Connecticut. Here a nurse learns the new techniques for treating certain illnesses and injuries in a high-pressure chamber.

The Navy Nurse Corps has its own Nursing Research Division to develop principles that will ultimately lead to improved patient care. In addition, nurses are assigned to such special projects as nuclear medicine and working with radio isotopes.

Being a Navy nurse is not just a job—it is a position of authority, and the many privileges add to its glamour.

Other Health Service Occupations

Although this chapter dealt mainly with the nursing profession, many other opportunities are available in the health service organizations. Most of them require the basic aptitudes and interests required for nursing and have training programs of two to four years' duration, depending upon whether you wish to seek the technician/assistant level or the bachelor's or advanced degrees.

Here they are:

Dental hygienist
Medical technologist
X-ray technician
Practical nurse
Psychiatric assistant
Dietitian

Physical therapist
Occupational therapist
Speech pathologist
Audiologist
Medical laboratory assistant

CHAPTER VIII

Secretarial and Clerical Jobs

Will computers and other mechanical devices ever replace secretaries? Never!

In my opinion, one of the most important groupings in most organizations is that of the secretarial and clerical occupations.

This chapter will deal with various clerical positions, but emphasis will be placed upon the secretary-stenographer, clerk-typist positions, since so many teenagers apply for and are hired for these types of job.

Why are these positions important? Let us look at the secretary:

She—or he—whatever the case may be is the "right hand" to a supervisor—whether she is secretary to the president of a large corporation or "Girl Friday" in a one-man, one-girl office. She is a combination of many things—the supervisor's sounding board for personal problems in addition to her basic duties of shorthand, typing, and various clerical tasks.

Normally a close working relationship exists between a supervisor and his secretary since they are greatly interdependent. This interdependence is based upon true loyalty, and, if this relationship does not exist, the working relationship is poor, and a lack of confidence results. If such is the case, there may be job disruptions to the point of not enjoying one's work. If such a situation cannot be remedied, the secretary should seek a job elsewhere.

Before going any further, I do not want to paint too glowing a picture and make every secretarial job sound like a Utopia or a top-notch position.

You must begin at the bottom of the ladder and work toward the top secretarial position. Since a company has only one president and few vice presidents, secretarial jobs at such levels are at a minimum. To acquire such a job requires great skills, maturity, excellent judgment, the ability to work independently, and the facility to make decisions—especially when the boss is away.

QUALIFICATIONS OF THE SECRETARY

Basic Skills

First of all come the basic mechanical skills of the position, typing, shorthand, and the ability to operate certain office machines (adding machine, duplicating equipment such as ditto machine, photocopier, etc.).

COURTESY CREATIVE PLAYTHINGS, INC.
PRINCETON, NEW JERSEY

The successful secretary possesses a special combination of personal qualities and technical skills.

Various degrees of proficiency are needed in the above skills depending upon the particular position. They will usually be governed by the size of the organization and the requirements of the supervisor.

Dictation and Shorthand

As far as shorthand is concerned, 80 words per minute is the average expected rate for the beginning secretary or stenographer. Note that we said the *average* rate. You may be expected to take letters at an even faster rate, but that would be an exception.

From experience, most supervisors dictate at a rate slower than is used in the tests you take in school or in the employment office. Why? In all likelihood your test was given from a phonograph record, or someone read the test to you. A supervisor will think out his letter while he is dictating, and will pause at intervals to collect his thoughts. If he sees that he is ahead of you, he will slow his pace to allow you to catch up.

A tip to beginners: If you get behind, do not be afraid to ask for clarification on a word or two—whether you need it or not—and that will allow you to catch up. Or simply say that you didn't catch a particular part of a sentence. A boss would rather have you ask the question at the time he is dictating than to have a typed letter brought to him with mistakes in it.

Every supervisor differs in the way he dictates. You will become accustomed to his style. Here are a few of the types you can expect:

The supervisor who dictates everything, working only from basic notes or sheer memory.

The one who writes out everything before he dictates because he is not sure of his thought patterns.

The supervisor who will dictate commas, paragraphs, periods, and all. Personally, I think this is a waste of time and not very flattering to the secretary, since she has been trained in these skills.

The one who will get halfway through a sentence or letter and ask you to finish it. (When you have reached this stage, you have arrived!)

Shorthand is a valuable skill; when applying for a job, be sure to find out ahead of time the amount of dictation that will be required. No secretary who has good shorthand skills should accept a job which does not call for this ability—unless she does not care to use her shorthand.

If you find that you take little dictation in your job, or your supervisor is away, practice the skill—from the radio or TV or from recordings of telephone messages. Or you could ask some one to read aloud to you from a book or newspaper. This is one skill that does not take long to lose. Some secretaries who take dictation daily and on an extensive basis find that they are not as sharp after a weekend, holiday, or vacation. This is true especially if you have reached the rate of 100 to 120 words per minute.

Taking dictation is only half the battle. Transcribing your notes is the proof! Regardless of how fast you jot down the symbols, the accurate, neatly typed finished product is the goal.

Make sure all words fit into the document logically and are correctly spelled and punctuated. Beginners frequently make the mistake of typing an entirely different word from the one dictated because the shorthand characters are nearly the same. For example, the word "similar" for "smaller." Make sure the words make sense before delivering the finished product. A lot of this comes through experience, but my purpose is to point these things out to you now so you can keep them in mind for your first position or employment test.

Typing

In applying for most secretarial, stenographic, or general typing positions, be prepared to take a test. What to expect?

You will be measured on two basic qualities—your accuracy and your speed. (See Chapter IV to determine the type of test you can expect.)

As to accuracy versus speed, most firms will lean toward the slow but more accurate typist as opposed to one who works rapidly and has little to show except errors. However, a minimum score must be attained, and you cannot work at such a slow pace that you completely sacrifice speed for accuracy. Sixty words per minute is an average rate for the beginner. Most people work faster and more accurately when well rested. Be sure to get a good night's rest before going for your tests.

A tip: Before taking the test, ask if you may practice a few minutes so you can become familiar with the typewriter.

Word processing machines are becoming standard equipment in offices. The skilled operator is in demand and highly paid.

Office Machines

Almost all clerical employees are expected to be able to operate basic office machines, the simplest being the adding machine or the photocopy machine. Dictating machines, dittos, comptometers, and mimeograph machines may be a little more complex.

Letter Writing and English Usage

A secretary should be able to compose a good letter. Many answers are routine, and a secretary who can handle such routine things can save her supervisor much time and inconvenience. Many offices have form letters with "canned" paragraphs, which the secretary can adjust to fit the particular occasion. Basic to the job are a good command of spelling, knowledge of grammar with emphasis on sentence structure, and a feel for paragraphing and punctuation.

In transcribing a letter, these last are vital, since it will be your job to rearrange the words dictated into the finished pattern.

Filing

You can expect as many filing systems as there are offices. Some supervisors are very possessive about their files and may go so far as to give you detailed information on where and how to file. Others will recognize the fact that you have been trained in this area and will allow you to develop your own system—as long as you can "deliver the goods" when asked. However, make sure that you develop a system that provides for cross-reference, especially if the matters to be filed are many and of a complicated nature. Being unable to locate a file within a reasonable amount of time can be embarrassing and will reflect upon your competency.

You may expect a test in this area regarding alphabetizing (see Chapter IV).

Personal Qualities

Every successful secretary must have topflight personal qualities in order to present the proper image or to perform successfully.

She or he is the "front" person in most offices and presents the first impression to outsiders. A secretary's treatment of a customer or other visitor could mean the success of a sale or some other advantage to the company. The same applies to her telephone manner.

How about your attitude and cooperation with fellow workers? You as a secretary will undoubtedly have to depend upon others to get your job done—other secretaries, clerks, the fellows in the mail room or duplicating room, the custodian or matron. Your attitude toward them will greatly influence their cooperation with you.

Oddly, statistics show that most people know their jobs, but the greatest failing of most employees is that they cannot get along with fellow employees. You must learn to be a team worker and carry your fair share of the load in the team effort.

Loyalty to Your Employer

If one is to work for a firm and make his livelihood with that organization, he must be loyal or seek employment elsewhere. The employee/employer relationship is one of mutual trust and cooperation. You must depend upon each other. However, it is important for you to remember that, in a tight job market, he can get along without you more readily than you can get along without him.

Poor Employee Attitudes and Work Habits

Below is a list of actions that can quickly make one unpopular in a work situation, with both the employer and your fellow employees:

(1) Pull a disappearing act when a team effort is needed.
(2) Receive personal phone calls or spend time on other personal business on company time.
(3) Be boisterous and noisy.
(4) Borrow money regularly from your fellow workers.
(5) Constantly prevail upon others for personal favors.
(6) Chew gum and snap it at every opportunity!
(7) Use crude and vulgar language.
(8) Fail to care for personal hygiene needs.
(9) Arrive late, leave early, and take the longest coffee breaks.
(10) Be away from desk when needed.
(11) Bring personal problems to office to discuss with one and all.
(12) Boast about prowess: "fast" girl—"ladies' man"—athletic accomplishments.
(13) Argue strongly over personal issues such as politics and make uncalled-for comments regarding race, color, and religion.

BOOKKEEPING AND ACCOUNTING POSITIONS

These positions can best be described as involving accuracy and a facility for numbers. All office clerical workers should have aptitudes in these areas. By this I do not mean only the knack for simple calculations, but true aptitude. Areas such as bookkeeping, accounting, payroll, taxes, banking, keypunch, and purchasing will require constant contact with figures.

Here you can expect simple arithmetic tests, number-checking tests, work checking, as described in Chapter IV.

CLERICAL AND RELATED OCCUPATIONS

Much of the following information is derived from the *Occupational Outlook Handbook* of 1976–77 and will give you an overall look at the various types of clerical and related occupations, along with other helpful data.

About 17,000,000 people were employed in clerical or some closely related work in 1978. A great many of these workers keep records and do other paperwork required in present-day offices. Others handle communications through mail, telephone, telegraph, and messenger services; attend to the shipping and receiving of merchandise; ring up sales on the cash registers of stores and restaurants; or do related work.

Clerical workers represent a wide variety of skills and experience. Included, for example, are title searchers and examiners in real-estate firms, and executive secretaries in business offices, as well as workers in occupations that can be entered with little specialized training or experience: messengers, file clerks, and others. For women, clerical occupations constitute a particularly large field of employment. More than half of all girls who go to work after completing high school find jobs in clerical and related occupations. Seven out of ten clerical workers are women.

By far the largest single group of clerical workers—one out of five—work as secretaries or stenographers. Bookkeepers and accounting clerks make up the next largest group.

Stenographers and secretaries are employed by public and private organizations of practically every size and type. A few—chiefly public stenographers and some reporting stenographers—are self-employed.

Particularly large numbers of stenographers and secretaries work for manufacturing firms, government agencies, schools and colleges, insurance companies, banks, and hospitals. Many, including technical stenographers and secretaries, are employed in the offices of physi-

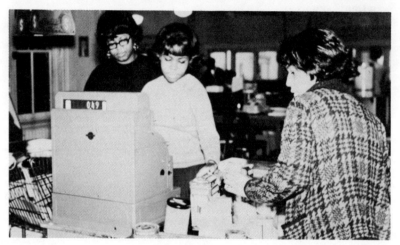

COURTESY OPPORTUNITIES INDUSTRIALIZATION CENTER, INC.
PHILADELPHIA, PENNSYLVANIA

Students learning retail sales techniques at the OIC in Philadelphia.

cians, attorneys, and other professional people. Stenographic and secretarial jobs for men tend to be concentrated in educational and other professional services, and in manufacturing and public administration. About three-fifths of the stenographers in the United States who specialize in shorthand reporting are men.

Bookkeepers and Accounting Clerks

More than 1,800,000 workers were employed in bookkeeping jobs in 1978, and 90 percent were women. The great majority of bookkeeping workers either do general bookkeeping or are accounting clerks. Some operate bookkeeping machines. Large numbers of bookkeeping workers are employed in retail stores, banks, insurance companies, and manufacturing firms of almost every kind.

Receptionists

It is estimated that about 500,000 receptionists were working in the United States in 1978. About one out of every three was a part-time worker who spent fewer than 35 hours a week on the job. More than 95 percent were women.

Although jobs for receptionists exist in practically every kind of establishment, about half of the persons in this occupation are employed in the offices of physicians, attorneys, and other professional people. Many others are employed by hospitals and educational institutions and still others by banks, insurance companies, real-estate offices, manufacturing concerns, and beauty shops.

The relatively small number of men who are employed as receptionists work principally in medical service and hospital jobs, in manufacturing, and in banking and credit agencies.

Cashiers

Cashiers work for business firms of all types and sizes. More than half are employed in grocery, drug, and other retail stores. Large numbers are also employed in restaurants, theaters, and in hotels and motels.

Most of these establishments and the other kinds of business that employ cashiers—wholesale houses and telephone companies, for example—are found in cities and in the shopping centers of heavily populated suburban areas, but some are in many small towns.

In 1978 more than 1,400,000 cashiers were employed in the United States. About half were part-time workers who spent fewer than 35 hours a week on the job, and about four out of five were women. More than half of all women cashiers work in food stores, restaurants, and department and general merchandise stores. The largest single group of men cashiers work in food stores such as supermarkets.

Office Machine Operators

About 750,000 people were employed as office machine operators in 1978. This total does not include more than 200,000 operators who run bookkeeping machines and electronic computer systems. About three-fourths of all office machine operators are women. Women outnumber men in practically all such jobs except those that involve the operation of tabulating machines.

Office machine operators are employed mainly in firms handling a large volume of record keeping and other paperwork. Consequently, a great many operators work in large cities where such firms are

COURTESY CREATIVE PLAYTHINGS, INC.
PRINCETON, NEW JERSEY

The various computer operations have created many jobs for high-school graduates.

usually situated. Approximately one-third of all office machine operators work for manufacturing companies. Others work for banks and insurance companies, government agencies, and wholesale and retail firms. Some office machine operators are employed in "service centers"—agencies that have various kinds of office machines and that contract to handle, for other firms lacking the equipment, such tasks as preparing monthly bills and mailing circulars to lists of prospective customers.

Electronic Computer Operating Personnel

The number of console and auxiliary equipment operators employed in 1978 was estimated at 600,000. Jobs for operating personnel are found chiefly in government agencies and in insurance companies, banks, wholesale and retail businesses, transportation and public utility companies, and manufacturing firms. Many operators are also employed in independent service organizations that process data for other firms on a fee basis.

Women held more than 90 percent of the keypunch jobs and nearly 45 percent of the console and auxiliary equipment jobs.

Telephone Operators

Almost 500,000 people were employed as telephone operators in 1978. Practically all were women.

Central office operators in telephone companies slightly outnumbered PBX operators in other types of establishment. Although PBX operators worked in establishments of all kinds, a particularly large number were employed in manufacturing plants, hospitals, schools, and department stores. Jobs for both central office and PBX operators tend to be concentrated in heavily populated areas. Nearly one-fifth of the total operators were employed in the New York, Chicago, and Los Angeles metropolitan areas, for example.

Shipping and Receiving Clerks

The number of shipping and receiving clerks in 1978 was estimated at more than 590,000. Two out of every three worked in manufacturing firms, and another fairly large group worked for wholesale houses or retail stores. The remainder were employed by transportation and freight-forwarding companies, and by many other kinds of business firm. About 75 percent of all shipping and receiving clerks are men.

Shipping and receiving clerks are employed in large factories, warehouses, and stores. The majority work in metropolitan areas, in which such establishments tend to be concentrated.

CHAPTER IX

The College Admission Interview

For some people, getting into college is a difficult, frustrating, endless experience, whereas others appear to gain entrance with very little effort except to go through the required formalities.

Why is this?

Those who enter with a minimum of trouble have prepared themselves over a period of years. Some may have done it with a planned program. Others simply do not realize that the good work they have done day by day over the years results in this great payoff. This preparation took the form of being a good student through regular, diligent study, getting along with classmates and teachers, being punctual, and being active and constructive in extracurricular activities.

To begin thinking about all these things in your senior year is too late. The time to begin is at least with the freshman year of high school. To wait until your senior year is a case of letting your past catch up with you.

With the competition of others attempting to get into college, you must face up to the fact that you may not be accepted at the college of your choice. It may be necessary for you to take the second, third, or fourth one on the list.

High-school performance is only one factor. You must pass the college screening—the tests and the personal interviews—assuming, of course, that you have access to the necessary money to put you through four years of college, or are prepared to help yourself by working part-time and during the summers.

High-School Student Inventory

Let us take a look at those qualities that are being sought in students by institutions of higher learning:

126

Motivation	Influence on others
Integrity	Leadership
Industry	Concern for others
Emotional stability	Co-curriculum activities
Initiative	Special projects
Responsibility	

Being accepted into college requires careful planning and a combination of many qualities.

Note that grades are not mentioned. Grades are basic and in most colleges come before anything else. If you lack the necessary grades, you won't get so far as to be considered for the other factors. Obviously you can see that the ratings of your teachers carry great weight.

What combinations of qualities are sought by most colleges?

First of all are the College Board exams, the early indications of whether students have the ability to be successful in college work. These are the PSAT (Preliminary Scholastic Aptitude Test) and SAT (Scholastic Aptitude Test). They are used *in combination with* your high-school academic record to predict your chances of success.

The PSAT is a several-hour multiple-choice test that measures verbal and mathematical abilities, word relationships, reading comprehension, and skill in interpreting and solving math problems.

The PSAT is not actually a college admission test. It is given during the junior year of high school, and in addition to being used as a guidance tool, is considered a "dry run" for the SAT, which is administered during the senior year.

The SAT is the more commonly used admission device. This battery of tests is three or more hours), but is similar in pattern to the PSAT.

Because of the wide variety of areas covered, cramming is of no value. The diligence—or lack of it—over the last ten or twelve years of school work will determine your score. By far the best preparation is to get a good night's sleep.

Various other tests are designed to measure your ability to do college work, for example, achievement tests—one-hour tests to determine what you have learned in various subject areas.

The ACT (American College Testing program) has the following sections:

1. Interpreting the student's high school record.
2. Completion of a Student Profile describing academic, extra-curricular, and vocational plans, plus other data to help with college counseling.
3. Four tests of 35 to 50 minutes each, designed to measure your ability to do college work. The test format is much the same as the SAT. Involved are multiple-choice tests in English usage, mathematics usage, social studies, reading, and the Natural Sciences Reading section.

It is recommended that you begin to think about the tests at the beginning of your junior year. Taking the tests for the first time in your junior year will give you an idea of what to expect regarding the types of questions asked and their content. You may take them again in your senior year.

Since most of the tests are of the multiple-choice variety, check Chapter IV to determine your approach. All types of tests, how to take them, and how they are scored are covered there.

Describe Yourself

This will be asked with the purpose of determining some of your goals and objectives as well as how clearly you express yourself. You may be asked for several hundred words in your own handwriting. I cannot help much in this regard if your handwriting is poor, except to say: Take your time or print your information carefully.

The Personal Interview

During the personal interview, the above questions will be posed in order to determine some of the following:

Sense of humor
Self-confidence
Concern for and ability to work with others
Ability to take criticism
Initiative
Dependability
Leadership
Can you study independently?
Can you budget your time (you'll be on your own)?
Can you be entrusted with this life of responsibility and accountability?
Can you make sacrifices—forsake a football game or dance in order to study?

Check Chapter II on applying for a job and completing the application. It will present even more tips on the qualities that are being sought by the colleges.

College Admission Forms

The college admission form is used in much the same way as an employment application. The college must make the best selection possible, as the turnover or dropout rate can be compared to an employer losing employees.

If you cannot hold your own in college and are forced to drop out, you have usurped a spot that could have been used by someone who might have made it.

Here are some of the points that college admission officers will stress when screening applicants for admission. They are not too unlike the information requested on employment applications. You will find the familiar questions for data such as age, address, high school, Social Security number, any past employment. Let us look at other questions and why they are asked.

Will You Live on Campus?

Many schools require freshmen to live on campus so they may make the adjustment to college life with as few interruptions as possible. If you are off campus, where will you study and when? What outside influences will there be? With whom will you room? Will you have suitable living quarters?

Will You Commute to College?

What is the commuting distance to the college from where you will be living? If you do not have the use of a car, is public transportation available? How would the transportation dovetail with your class schedule?

Must You Work to Defray College Expenses?

Very few young people going to college today have a "free ride." Nearly everyone does some kind of work to help out.

How many years must you work? How will your work schedule tie in with your class schedule? Will you have time for proper study and sleep?

If you need financial help for college expenses, many funds are available. Check with your guidance counselor. All colleges have printed material on this subject that they will furnish along with your application.

What Were Your High-School Activities?

This question will be found on all applications. Colleges seek well-rounded students who can adjust quickly and thus become a part of the "college community." Do not undersell yourself. It does not mean that you must pursue the same interests in college, but they can be determining factors in gaining entrance:

Sports—Freshman, junior varsity, or varsity. Perhaps your school had an active intramural program.

Clubs—Yearbook, cheerleading, 4-H Club, choral groups, fund drives, booster clubs, band, dramatics, science clubs, and other academic groups.

Outside activities—Be sure to list activities outside of school such as church work, Scouts, community and civic activities, "Y" groups. Do not forget the early years of high school, the freshman and sophomore years.

Honors—These weigh heavily in the area of leadership, dependability, and initiative. Besides academic and scholarship honors, mention such items as sports captain, club offices held, articles written for the yearbook or newspaper.

Special interests—The newspapers, books, and magazines you read in order to broaden yourself.

However, if you were not inclined to activities and if you had to work to earn money, please note this. These points can carry as much weight.

Why Did You Choose Our College?

This will be a standard question, and you should be prepared to be specific.

What is the curriculum, the size, placement of its graduates? Is it near home, far from home, co-ed? What are the chances for graduate-school admission?

Athletes applying for or being approached for scholarships should seek the advice of coaches regarding such special questions as: amount of scholarship help, freedom to select courses, tutorial services. Will scholarships be honored if the athlete is injured? What about classes lost because of travel? What about book costs, room, board, laundry, allowances?

What Course Do You Intend to Pursue?

A most important question. Here again, be specific. Is it for life's work, preparation for professional school? Be prepared with your answer.

Past Employment

Here again the school is seeking information as to the all-around individual. Do you know what it is to work? Can you work with others? Did you have to earn your own spending money? How did you spend the money you earned? Did you save it, or "blow it" on something without meaning?

When Is the Best Time to Apply?

With the great competition today for college acceptance, you must be alert as to application deadlines. This is especially important if you are applying to several colleges with varying application methods.

At the end of your junior year in high school you should begin planning in earnest. Even before that time, your parents may be interested in taking weekend trips to look at campuses in which you might be interested. Obtain sample applications and catalogues and other information from your guidance counselor (he should be your expert) and begin developing your time frame.

Write for applications at the end of your junior year or during the summer before your senior year in order to have ample time to study the forms and to complete them properly.

Most colleges set a *deadline date* of February 1 of your senior year for sending in applications. This *is* the deadline date, and many procrastinators will be sending in their applications at the last minute. Get your bid in much before that. Most colleges would like to have senior grades for the first marking period included with the application. This is usually between November 15 and 30. Get your applications all out before Christmas vacation starts so you can relax and enjoy your free time.

If you have completed much of your high school requirements, you may want to go to college early. Check with your counselor the possibilities of entering college after your junior year or in January of your senior year.

Another little tip on applying: Since the college will receive thousands of applications, all the same color and size, do something to make yours stand out from the rest. If you have a special identifying stationery, use it. If not, use a different color of paper for your letter of transmittal. Do not go too far out or the Admissions Office will remember you for this reason only.

If you apply at several schools and are accepted at more than one, the elimination process may become tricky. As a matter of ethics, if you should be accepted at a school you find you do not wish to attend, notify them immediately so someone else can be "slotted" in your place. It is difficult to know what to do when you have not as yet heard from the school of your choice and you have been accepted elsewhere. It is a time for soul-searching and patience. Take each day as it comes.

The interview itself will be similar to the employment interview except that at some schools you may have to appear before a screening board of several people.

Should your parents attend the initial interview with the Admissions Office with you? Some schools encourage this in order to find out more about your background. Personally, I do not believe in this, for many parents can talk the son or daughter out of admission—without intending to, of course. By the time you have graduated from high school, you should be able to handle this aspect of your future.

After personal contact with the college, a follow-up letter of thanks is always in order. It demonstrates a thoughtful, courteous, and businesslike approach.

Perhaps by practicing all of the above, your wait for admission may not seem too long.

CHAPTER X

Employment Laws: Rights and Regulations

The message in this chapter will give the young worker and the guidance counselor insight into the various federal and state work regulations and provide them with some idea of workers' rights as they pertain to wages, working conditions, overtime provisions, child-labor restrictions, unionism, equal pay, employment opportunity, and similar issues.

Child-Labor Provisions

The teenager and other youthful workers should have at their fingertips a summary of the various types of job suited for young persons as permitted under federal and state laws. They will need to be familiar with this information in order to know where to apply for jobs, how to apply, and what wage level to expect.

The following information is derived from the Guide on Child Labor Provisions of the U.S. Department of Labor, and outlines the various facets of the Fair Labor Standards Act of 1966. This is commonly referred to as the Federal Wage–Hour Law and covers employees engaged in interstate or foreign commerce.

Sixteen is the magic age for gainful employment and is the basic minimum age for employment. At 16, young people may be employed in *any* occupation other than a nonagricultural occupation declared hazardous by the Secretary of Labor. No other restrictions are made. Unless contrary to state or local law, young people of this age may be employed *during school hours* for any number of hours, and during any periods of time.

Further, 16 is the minimum age for employment in an agricultural occupation declared hazardous by the Secretary of Labor at any time. It is also the minimum age for employment in agriculture during the hours schools are in session in the district where the minor lives while working.

Fourteen is the minimum age for specified occupations *outside* school hours. The purpose of this regulation is to limit 14- and 15-year-olds to certain conditions that will not interfere with their schooling, health, or well-being.

For instance, during school hours, 14- and 15-year-old minors may *not* be employed

(1) before 7 A.M. or after 7 P.M. (except 9 P.M. June 1 through Labor Day).
(2) more than three hours per day on school days.
(3) more than eighteen hours per week—in school weeks.
(4) more than eight hours per day—on nonschool days.
(5) more than forty hours per week—in nonschool weeks.

Eighteen is the minimum age for employment in nonagricultural occupations declared hazardous by the Secretary of Labor.

Those are the general rules, with certain exceptions—such as in the case of training programs conducted under federal sponsorship or such occupations as selling magazines. However, in these instances, special permission must be obtained from school principals or other authorities.

The Fair Labor Standards Act covers employees engaged in interstate or foreign commerce and are more restrictive than state laws. Your school authorities can help you with state laws.

In order to bar child labor and to provide employers with guidelines on the hiring of youth, the various states have programs of "working papers." Before school-age youths may be employed in certain types of work, they must receive a clearance from school authorities. (See typical example of working papers schedule in this chapter.)

PERMITTED OCCUPATIONS FOR 14- AND 15-YEAR-OLD MINORS IN RETAIL, FOOD SERVICE, AND GASOLINE SERVICE ESTABLISHMENTS

Fourteen- and 15-year-old minors may be employed in:

(1) office and clerical work (including operation of office machines).

(2) cashiering, selling, modeling, art work, work in advertising departments, window trimming, and comparative shopping.

(3) price marking and tagging by hand or machine.

(4) bagging and carrying out customers' orders.

(5) errand and delivery work by foot, bicycle, and public transportation.

(6) cleanup work, including the use of vacuum cleaners and floor waxers, and maintenance of grounds, but not including the use of power-driven mowers or cutters.

(7) kitchen work and other work involved in preparing and serving food and beverages, including the operation of machines and devices used in the performance of such work, such as, but not limited to, dishwashers, toasters, dumbwaiters, popcorn poppers, milk shake blenders, and coffee grinders.

(8) work in connection with cars and trucks if confined to the following:

Dispensing gasoline and oil.

Courtesy service.

Car cleaning, washing, and polishing.

Other occupations permitted by this section.

(9) cleaning vegetables and fruits, and wrapping, sealing, labeling, weighing, pricing, and stocking goods when performed in areas physically separate from areas where meat is prepared for sale, and outside freezers or meat coolers.

In Any Other Place of Employment

Fourteen- and 15-year-old minors may be employed in any occupation except the excluded occupations listed below:

Fourteen- and 15-year-old minors may *not* be employed in:

(1) any manufacturing occupation.

(2) any mining occupation.

(3) processing occupations (except in a retail, food service, or gasoline service establishment in those specific occupations expressly permitted there in accordance with the foregoing list).

(4) occupations requiring the performance of any duties in workrooms or workplaces where goods are manufactured, mined,

or otherwise processed (again, except to the extent expressly permitted in retail, food service, or gasoline service establishments in accordance with the foregoing list).

(5) public messenger service.

(6) operation or tending of hoisting apparatus or any power-driven machinery (other than office machines and machines in retail, food service, and gasoline service establishments specified in the foregoing list as machines that such minors may operate in such establishments).

(7) any occupations found and declared to be hazardous.

(8) occupations in connection with:
    (a) transportation of persons or property by rail, highway, air, on water, pipeline or other means.
    (b) warehousing and storage.
    (c) communications and public utilities.
    (d) construction (including repair), except office or sales work in connection with these occupations (not performed on transportation media or at the actual construction site).

(9) any of the following occupations in a retail, food establishment, or gasoline service establishment:
    (a) Work performed in or about boiler or engine rooms.
    (b) Work in connection with maintenance or repair of the establishment, machines, or equipment.
    (c) Outside window washing that involves working from window sills, and all other work requiring the use of ladders, scaffolds, or their substitutes.
    (d) Cooking (except at soda fountains, lunch counters, snack bars, or cafeteria serving counters) and baking.
    (e) Occupations that involve operating, setting up, adjusting, cleaning, oiling, or repairing power-driven food slicers and grinders, food choppers and cutters, and bakery-type mixers.
    (f) Work in freezers and meat coolers, and all work in preparation of meats for sale (except wrapping, sealing, labeling, weighing, pricing and stocking when performed in other areas).
    (g) Loading and unloading goods to and from trucks, railroad cars, or conveyors.

(h) All occupations in warehouses except office and clerical work.

Age Certificates

An employer must protect himself from unintentional violation of the minimum age provisions by obtaining and keeping on file an age or employment certificate for each minor employed, showing the minor to be of the age established for the occupation in which he is employed. Employers are expected to obtain such a certificate and have it on file before the minor starts work.

Age or employment certificates, sometimes called work permits or *working papers,* issued under state child labor laws are accepted as proof of age in almost every state, the District of Columbia, and Puerto Rico. Special arrangements for proof of age have been made in Alaska. In four states—Idaho, Mississippi, South Carolina, and Texas—federal certificates of age are issued by the Wage and Hour and Public Contracts Divisions.

Age certificates have the twofold purpose of (1) protecting minors from harmful employment as defined by the child labor provisions of the act; and (2) protecting employers from unintentional violations of the minimum age provisions of the act by furnishing them with reliable proof of age for minors employed in their establishments. This protection is specifically authorized by the act.

To make sure that the minors in their employ are of legal age under the act, employers are urged to obtain an age certificate for every minor claiming to be under 18 before employing him in any occupation.

The age certificate protects the employer only if it shows the minor to be of the legal age for the occupation in which he is employed.

Every state has a child labor law, and all but one have compulsory school attendance laws. *Whenever a state standard differs from a federal standard, the higher standard must be observed.*

The following page displays an example of working papers.

You can readily see that a knowledge of the Fair Labor Standards Act is of great importance both to employers and employees. The basic rule for coverage of the child labor provisions is to determine whether the employers of an organization are engaged in interstate or foreign commerce. If such is the case, they are covered.

Employees engaged in interstate or foreign commerce are covered.

This includes, among others, workers in the telephone, telegraph, radio, television, importing, exporting, and transportation industries. It also includes employees in distributing industries, such as wholesalers who handle goods moving in interstate or foreign commerce, as well as workers who order, receive, or keep records of such goods; and clerical and other workers who regularly use the mails, telephone, and telegraph for interstate or foreign communications.

To confuse you further: There are exemptions from the law in which child labor provisions do not apply. For example, children under 16 employed by their parents in agriculture or in nonagricultural occupations other than manufacturing or mining occupations declared hazardous for minors under 18.

Children under 16 employed by other than their parents in agriculture, if the occupation has not been declared hazardous, and the employment is outside the hours schools are in session in the district where the minor lives while working.

Children employed as actors or performers in motion picture, theatrical, radio, or television productions.

Children engaged in the delivery of newspapers to the consumer.

Homemakers engaged in the making of wreaths composed principally of holly, pine, cedar, or other evergreens (including the harvesting of the evergreens).

Now we will zero in on the 16- and 17-year-olds. The Department of Labor has seventeen Hazardous Occupations Orders for minors between 16 and 18 (also minors 14 and 15). They are:

(1) Occupations in or about plants or establishments manufacturing or storing explosives or articles containing explosive components.
(2) Occupations of motor-vehicle driver and outside helper.
(3) Coal-mine occupations.
(4) Logging occupations and occupations in the operation of any sawmill, lath mill, shingle mill, or cooperage-stock mill.
(5) Occupations involved in the operation of power-driven wood-working machines.
(6) Occupations involving exposure to radioactive substances and to ionizing radiations.
(7) Occupations involved in the operation of elevators and other power-driven hoisting apparatus.

VACATION EMPLOYMENT CERTIFICATE NO. . . . .

(Issued only for a minor between 14 and 18 years of age who has complied with the requirements of The Child Labor Law, approved August 23, 1961.)

(Issued also to male minors, ages 12 and 13, employed as "Caddies" — Act 282, effective September 10, 1961.)

NAME AND ADDRESS OF PARENT OR GUARDIAN	DATE OF BIRTH OF MINOR			FIRST NAME OF MINOR	LAST NAME OF MINOR
	Month	Day	Year		

KIND OF EVIDENCE OF AGE ACCEPTED AND FILED | RESIDENCE OF MINOR

PLACE OF BIRTH—COUNTRY | SIGNATURE OF MINOR

DESCRIPTION OF MINOR (INDICATE BY X)

SEX: Male Female EYES: Dark Brown Light Brown Gray Black HAIR: Black Brown Blond Red

Distinguishing Physical Characteristics . . . .

Know all men that I, being the person authorized by law to issue employment certificates, hereby certify that the above-named minor personally appeared before me and has been examined and has presented all the credentials required by the several sections of the Pennsylvania Child Labor Law, that these credentials have been approved and filed in this office, that this certificate is approved by me and has been signed by the minor in my presence.

This certificate authorizes . . . .

(Name of Member, Superintendent, or Manager)

. . . . to employ the

(Name of Firm)   (Street or R. F. D.)   (Post Office)

above-named minor in accordance with the provisions of the law in the capacity of . . . .

(Occupation of Minor)

Issued { at . . . .

(Street or R. F. D.)   (Post Office)   . . . .

(Signature of issuing officer)

on . . . . , 19 . . . . . .

(Date)   (School District)   (Official title)

Form PICA-31 (VEC)
350M 1-67   (Over)

IMPORTANT: This certificate does not authorize employment contrary to the provisions of the Fair Labor Standards Act.

—COMMONWEALTH OF PENNSYLVANIA
DEPARTMENT OF PUBLIC EDUCATION

The Employment Certificate or "working papers" are necessary for minors who wish to work at selected jobs.

(8) Occupations involved in the operation of power-driven metal-forming, -punching, and -shearing machines.

(9) Occupations in connection with mining, other than coal.

(10) Occupations involving slaughtering, meat packing, or processing or rendering.

(11) Occupations involved in the operation of certain power-driven bakery machines.

(12) Occupations involved in the operation of certain power-driven paper-products machines.

(13) Occupations involved in the manufacture of brick, tile, kindred products.

(14) Occupations involved in the operation of circular saws, handsaws, and guillotine shears.

(15) Occupations involved in wrecking, demolition, and ship-breaking operations.

(16) Occupations involved in roofing operations.

(17) Occupations in excavation operations.

What we have given you here are the general categories. It is suggested that you consult with your guidance counselor or USES representative for detailed information on the above categories and on exceptions such as apprentices and student-learners.

The following U.S. Department of Labor information should prove helpful to young job seekers and to adults who are seeking wage and hour guidelines. "The Handy Reference Guide to the Fair Labor Standards Act" is the source of these guidelines.

The Fair Labor Standards Act of 1938, as amended, establishes minimum wage, maximum hours, overtime pay, equal pay, and child labor standards for covered employment, unless a specific exemption applies.

The 1966 amendments to the Fair Labor Standards Act of 1938 provide coverage for many additional workers and increase the minimum wages for others already subject to the law.

The new amendments, effective February 1, 1967, include broader definitions of the businesses that are subject to the act, and the elimination or revision of some of the exemptions previously in the act. Among other things, they extend the Fair Labor Standards Act to include more retail and service firms and establish minimum wage requirements for certain farm workers and other employees.

Prior to the 1966 amendments, the Fair Labor Standards Act applied only to employees individually engaged in interstate or foreign commerce and to those employed in certain large enterprises. Those employees who were previously covered by the act are still subject to it and its amendments. Unless specifically exempt, newly covered employees will be subject to the wage and hour standards for newly covered employment included in the 1966 amendments.

The following information is extracted directly from the *Handy Reference Guide to the Fair Standards Act* and is presented for use by young readers and counselors.

Minimum Wage Provisions Extended

Among the employees to whom minimum wage provisions have been extended by removal of exemption are employees in certain hotels, motels, restaurants, and other retail or service establishments, employees of taxicab companies, and additional transit companies, certain farm workers, employees of country elevators in the "area of production," cotton-ginning employees, and certain fruit and vegetable transportation employees.

Exemptions from Minimum Wage and Overtime Provisions

Employees of certain seasonal amusement or recreational establishments; of motion picture theaters; of certain small newspapers; switchboard operators of small telephone companies; seamen employed on other than American vessels; and employees engaged in fishing operations.

Farm workers employed by an employer who did not use more than 500 man-days of farm labor in any calendar quarter of the preceding calendar year; and employees engaged in certain operations relating to specified agricultural commodities.

Exemptions from Overtime Requirements Only

Certain higher-paid commission employees of retail or service establishments; salesmen, mechanics, and parts men primarily engaged in selling or servicing automobiles, trucks, trailers, farm implements, or aircraft, employed by nonmanufacturing establishments primarily engaged in the business of selling such vehicles to ultimate purchasers.

Employees of railroads and air carriers; drivers of taxicabs; seamen on American vessels; certain employees of motor carriers; and local delivery drivers paid on a trip rate basis or other delivery payment plan meeting prescribed conditions.

Announcers, news editors, and chief engineers of certain nonmetropolitan broadcasting stations.

Workweek

The workweek is the term applied to a period of 168 hours during seven consecutive 24-hour periods. The workweek may begin any day of the week or at any hour as established by the employer. Employment for two or more workweeks cannot be averaged out for the sake of overtime or minimum wages except under prescribed conditions, as in the case of seamen of American vessels and employees of hospitals. Employee coverage, compliance with the wage payment requirements, and the application of most exemptions are determined on the workweek basis.

Hours Worked

Any employee subject to the act must be paid in accordance with its provisions for all hours worked during the workweek. In general, "hours worked" includes all the time an employee is required to be on duty, or on the employer's premises, or at other prescribed places of work, and any other additional time he is required or permitted to work for the employer.

Tips

Tips received by a tipped employee may, within the prescribed limits, be considered by the employer as part of the wages of the employee. Wage credit permitted for such tips as the employer may determine may not exceed 50 percent of the applicable minimum rate beginning January 1, 1978; 45 percent is the minimum top credit beginning January 1, 1979, and 40 percent effective January 1, 1980. A "tipped" employee is a worker engaged in an occupation in which he customarily and regularly receives more than $30 a month in tips.

Employer-Furnished Facilities

The reasonable cost or fair value of board, lodging, and other facilities provided as determined by the Wage and Hour and Public Contracts Divisions' Administrator may be considered as part of the employee's wages.

How to Compute Overtime Pay

Overtime pay must be paid at a rate of not less than 1½ times the employee's regular rate of pay for each hour worked in a workweek in excess of the maximum hours applicable to the type of employment in which the employee is engaged.

The "regular rate" may be more than the minimum wage; it may not be less. Except for certain types of payments, an employee's regular rate includes all payments made by the employer to or on behalf of that employee. Assuming that the employee receives no compensation other than that stated, here are some typical cases based, for example only, on a maximum workweek of 40 hours:

1. *Hourly Rate*—The regular rate of pay for an employee paid by the hour is his hourly rate. When he works more than 40 hours in a workweek, he is due at least 1½ times his regular rate for each hour over 40.

   Example: An employee is paid $3.80 an hour; this is his regular rate. If he worked a 44-hour workweek, he would be entitled to at least 1½ times $3.80, or $5.70, for each hour over 40. His pay for the week would be $152 for the first 40 hours plus $22.80 for the 4 hours overtime, or a total of $174.80.

EQUAL EMPLOYMENT OPPORTUNITY

Equality in job seeking, training, and pay levels received its birth during the 1960's. The economic and social status of the black has advanced at a much faster pace than the status of other elements of the population—and rightfully so.

Some of this has been brought about by legislation, pressure from ethnic groups, and the voluntary efforts of many employers who realize that minority groups are great sources of untapped manpower.

In July, 1961, a significant event occurred in American industry when the heads of nine major corporations met with the late President John F. Kennedy and set forth their voluntary "Plans for Progress," reaffirming their continuance of nondiscrimination in employment. In this group were:

RCA Corp.	General Electric Company
Boeing Company	North American Aviation, Inc.
Douglas Aircraft Co. Inc.	United Aircraft Corporation
Western Electric, Inc.	The Martin Company
Lockheed Aircraft Corporation	

Although these firms were primarily electronic and aircraft companies, today organizations representing varied business and geographic locations are part of this voluntary effort.

Any good business now knows the buying potential of minority

COURTESY OPPORTUNITIES INDUSTRIALIZATION CENTER, INC.
PHILADELPHIA, PENNSYLVANIA

Fair employment practices provide equal job opportunities for all.

groups, and it behooves them to cultivate this purchasing power through good employment practices and business techniques.

A federal agency, the Equal Employment Opportunity Commission (EEOC), has been established to monitor employment practices and has contributed greatly toward the program. Similarly, state agencies have been formed to insure equality.

Further, every program administered by the Department of Labor is covered by the various provisions of the Civil Rights Act of 1964. Individuals who are covered and have complaints of discrimination may file written complaints with the U.S. Secretary of Labor within ninety days of the alleged discrimination. Private employees may file complaints with the EEOC as well.

Basically, the areas of discrimination concern race, color, age, religion, sex, or national origin. However, in filing such claims, the complainant needs to be specific and accurate regarding names, dates, and offices, and other necessary details of the alleged discriminatory acts.

Another basic right of which most veterans are aware is the Veteran's Reemployment Rights. Individuals separating from the armed forces receive this information. It may also be obtained at a Veterans Administration office. The main items covered are rights to your old job, benefits that have accrued while you were away, job status, and pay upon your return.

Equal pay laws state that employers shall not discriminate between employees on the basis of sex by paying wages to any employee at a rate less than the rate at which he pays wages to employees of the opposite sex for work under comparable conditions for jobs that require comparable skills.

Further, except in cases in which sex is a bona fide occupational qualification (attendant in a women's sauna bath, for example), employers must provide equal employment opportunity to both sexes. The advancements in equal opportunity for sexes needs no further word. The movement speaks for itself.

LABOR UNIONS

The young job seeker needs to have at his fingertips the basic information about labor unions. He must be familiar with the types of unions, membership requirements, union dues, working contracts, state and federal laws, and other issues that may affect his working conditions, promotional opportunities, security, and certain wages.

The U.S. Department of Labor "Directory of National and International Labor Unions in the United States" provides useful information by listing the various national, international, and state labor organizations as well as developments that have occurred regarding structure and membership.

Union Membership Figures

To give you some idea of membership, the following information from the directory shows that in 1978 the membership of national unions and employee associations headquartered in the United States was 21,456,000 as compared with 19,166,000 in 1968. Organizing efforts among government workers and other public employees was mainly responsible for the growth.

In proportion to the total labor force, the downward movement of union membership has reversed. On the other hand, union membership has not kept pace with the growth of employment in non-agricultural establishments, which more closely approximates the area of potential organization.

State membership figures for all unions in the United States compiled by the Bureau of Labor Statistics showed that the combined membership of three states included one out of three members: New York had 3,215,000; California had 2,607,000; Pennsylvania, 1,849,000.

More than 200,000 labor agreements, exclusive of supplements and welfare and pension plans, were negotiated or in effect in 1978 for national and international unions.

On the distaff side, nearly 4,291,200 members, slightly more than 20 percent of all members in 1978, were women. Interestingly, this was an increase of 300,000 women in the 3-year period.

Rather than list page upon page of names of the various unions, we will rank in broad percentage categories industry groupings and division shown in order of degree of union organization:

75 percent and over
1. Ordnance
2. Transportation
3. Transportation equipment
4. Contract construction

50 percent to less than 75 percent
5. Electrical machinery
6. Food and kindred products
7. Primary metals
8. Mining
9. Telephone and telegraph
10. Paper
11. Petroleum
12. Tobacco manufactures

13. Apparel
14. Fabricated metals
15. Manufacturing
16. Stone, clay, and glass products
17. Federal Government

25 percent to less than 50 percent
18. Printing, publishing
19. Leather
20. Rubber
21. Furniture
22. Machinery
23. Lumber
24. Chemicals
25. Electric, gas utilities

Less than 25 percent
26. Nonmanufacturing
27. Government
28. Instruments
29. Textile mill products
30. State government
31. Local government
32. Service
33. Trade
34. Agricultural and fishing
35. Finance

		Membership (exclusive of Canada) as a percentage of:			
		Total labor force		*Employees in nonagricultural establishments*	
Year	*Total union membership*	*Number (thousands)*	*Percent union members*	*Number (thousands)*	*Percent union members*
1961	16,303	73,031	22.3	54,042	30.2
1966	17,940	78,893	22.7	63,864	28.1
1970	19,381	85,903	22.6	70,920	27.3
1974	20,199	93,240	21.7	78,413	25.8

Compulsory Membership

When applying for a job, especially in manufacturing firms, you should be prepared to join a union. The "union shop" provision of bargaining agreements (contracts) stipulates that all organized employees working in the particular firm must belong to the union. This is a negotiated item between the union and the employer, whereby the union feels that people who benefit from the union's efforts should share the responsibility and costs of membership in its organization.

Unions regard the contract as a sign of industrial democracy at work. It represents a voice in the hours, wages, and working conditions of the establishment. These hours, wages, and working conditions are mutually agreed upon during collective bargaining sessions, commonly known as negotiations.

Some states have labor legislation in the form of "right-to-work" laws that prohibit the "union shop," and the worker makes his own decision whether to join the union.

As a middle ground between the "right-to-work" laws and the "union shop" is legislation in the form of the "agency shop." This stipulates that employees may not be obliged to join a particular union, but they must pay union dues in order to help defray costs. The philosophy expounded here is that if you are to enjoy the benefits of the union's endeavors, then you must be willing to help support the costs of obtaining the benefits.

When employed in a "union shop," you can expect to pay an initiation fee plus monthly dues. These are usually deducted from your paycheck by means of the "check-off" system.

Further, when employed in a union shop, you will ordinarily serve a probationary work period—usually thirty days—before you need to join the union. The purpose of this trial period is to determine whether you can meet the qualifications of the job. If the employer deems your work satisfactory after this period, you will begin to accumulate union "seniority" or security.

The majority of union security clauses are "union-shop" clauses. However, some contracts may contain "closed-shop" provisions. The employer usually hires persons who are already union members rather than probationary employees. This type of agreement is most common in the printing, construction, longshoring, and certain other trades.

Unions are a fact of life and are here to stay. If you job hunt, be prepared to join such an organization as a condition of employment.

CHAPTER XI

Jobs of Tomorrow: The Decade Ahead

We are going to devote some space to talking about the kinds of job that will exist in the future—in five to ten or more years. Although the subject of available jobs is not our main topic, perhaps of we dedicate a few words to the future here and now, you will know what to expect and how to prepare for that interview of the future, when you might be seeking your first truly permanent job.

In planning your future, you will need to know the composition of the work force and the occupational trends. People will need to gear their education and training to the changing economy and the new types of jobs that will present themselves. The person who is graduating from junior high school this year may be gainfully employed ten years from now in an occupation that does not exist today.

One area of concern that is posing interesting problems for economists and sociologists is the problem of leisure time. The "problem" stems from the fact that the four-day week may become a reality during the next decade and the concern is, "Are we prepared to cope with this leisure time?"

It is anticipated that leisure will not truly become leisure, but will encourage people to take second jobs. They will "moonlight" not only to fill an excess of free time, but also to raise their standard of living so they will be able to buy material things they would not otherwise have been able to afford. The part-time worker who averages about thirteen hours per week in this extra job is described in greater detail in Chapter V.

Another facet of this new "problem" is that people find they become bored while vacationing for long periods of time. For example, the steel industry has a plan whereby long-service employees earn as many as thirteen weeks of vacation a year. Studies have shown that after several weeks of traveling, painting the house, or putting on that home addition, most men begin to think about returning to their jobs—or just doing something constructive rather than just loafing.

In regard to this leisure time, new industries or expanded ones

151

will develop to capitalize on this new employment market. Here are a few businesses that revolve around recreation expansion: hunting, fishing, skiing, boating and related sports and activities, camping, mobile homes, publishing houses (more reading time and greater literacy), travel industries, hotel and motel services, such special areas as photography, radio and television, motion picture and recording companies. Service industries will grow because people will seek such services (educational services, personal services such as beauty shops, men's hair salons).

Now let us analyze the overall picture of tomorrow's job to get a better idea of what you can expect in the way of specific types of occupations that will appear and how to prepare for them.

The *Occupational Outlook Handbook* provides useful information in this area. Much of the information in this chapter comes from that source. The handbook is a publication of the U.S. Department of Labor.

In analyzing the future employment market we must review losses as well as gains in employment. For example, labor-saving devices have accounted for declines in agricultural development. However, in the building trades, employment has increased.

Employment Growth 1974–85

Industries	Percentage Rate of Growth
Services	50
Government	35
Contract construction	21
Trade	22
Finance, insurance, real estate	35
Transportation, public utilities	11
Manufacturing	12
Mining	17
Agriculture	32

It is expected that a 20 percent overall increase in total employment will take place over the next decade with growth in those areas shown above. The greatest number of workers will continue to be employed in manufacturing, but employment in manufacturing is expected to grow only half as fast as the other areas.

The future employment level of individual industries will be the most important factor in determining what the occupational requirements will be. For example, the insurance business, which employs a large number of clerical, sales, and other white-collar workers, differs greatly from the construction industry, which primarily employs blue-collar workers: carpenters, electricians, and laborers. As a result, a sharp change in the total employment of the construction industry will have a great effect on the requirements for blue-collar workers. Thus it follows that, if employment in the insurance industry changes sharply, requirements for workers in white-collar occupations will be greatly affected.

The second factor that influences the trend in occupational employment is the changing occupational structure within the industry itself.

Semiskilled workers are the largest occupational group, which represents an important source of work for new young male workers: factory assemblers, inspectors, machine operators and apprentices, truck, taxicab, and bus drivers.

The second and third largest occupational groups, clerical and service workers, are a major source of work for women. Craftsmen, the skilled worker category, make up the fourth largest group. The next largest or fifth group comprises professional workers, most of whom have had some college training.

Within each occupational group, a wide spread of jobs requires differing levels of education and skill. For instance, among professional and related workers are nuclear physicists as well as athletes; and among service workers are FBI agents and household workers. Similarly, sales workers include technical sales representatives with engineering backgrounds as well as retail salesclerks.

In general, employment growth will be fastest among those occupations requiring the most education and training to enter.

Employment in professional and related occupations will show the fastest growth over the next ten years—twice as fast as overall employment. Those occupations generally require the most formal educational preparation to qualify for employment.

To be a high-school graduate has become standard for American workers. Employers are seeking people with higher levels of education because jobs are more complex than they used to be and require higher levels of skill. That is quite evident in jobs in the clerical, sales, and service fields.

More jobs will require extensive education and training.

FUTURE MANPOWER REQUIREMENTS

Teaching is a large profession and, like nursing, represents a major source of employment for women. Engineering is the major field of professional employment for men. Altogether, nearly 13,000,000 persons work in these and other professional and technical fields.

Scientific and engineering employment is expected to grow faster than that of the professional group as a whole. The growth rate for scientists is likely to be greater than that of engineers. Technicians who assist engineers and scientists will also show a rapid rate of growth.

Growth Rate in Health Occupations

Position	Percent Increase 1970–1980
Medical technologists	102
Dental hygienists	80
Medical record librarians	50
Registered professional nurses	44
Medical X-ray technicians	44
Physicians	38
Dentists	30
Dental lab technicians	28
Dietitians and nutritionists	28
Veterinarians	12
Pharmacists	8

Clerical Occupations

About 15 million people are employed in clerical occupations. The field is also a major source of employment for young people.

Clerical workers represent a large variety of skills. This occupational group includes, for example, highly skilled workers such as title researchers and examiners in real-estate firms, and confidential secretaries in businesses of all kinds. It also includes occupations such as those of messenger and file clerk, which can be entered with little specialized training.

Technological changes and improvements in the field, which includes the use of computers, have reshaped the nature of the work of office-machine operators. Entirely new functions have been created, such as those performed by electronic computer personnel. Employment in those fields, though less numerous than among the traditional clerical occupations, is growing the fastest.

Through the mid-1980's the percent change in employment growth for clerical occupations is expected to be about 35 percent versus 1974.

It is interesting to note the unusual growth in computer and office-machine occupations and the lesser growth in the bookkeeping jobs. A direct effect is evident here because of automated techniques and less use for manual skills. It is clear that those with clerical skills and aptitudes need to think in terms of the data-processing and machine occupations.

Sales Occupations

About 6,000,000 persons are employed in sales occupations. Of this number, about one-fourth are employed on a part-time basis. Salesworkers employed in retail stores account for over one-half of the employment in the group. Most of the workers are women. Almost all persons employed outside the retail trade—in wholesale trade, manufacturing, insurance companies, real-estate firms, and other companies—are men.

In the 1974–85 period, employment in the sales group may rise by 20 percent. Most of that growth is likely to occur in occupations outside the retail field among real-estate salesmen, insurance agents, manufacturer's salesmen, and others.

Skilled Occupations

Construction workers, mechanics and repairmen, and machinists make up the majority of the country's skilled work force. New entrants into those fields generally have at least a high-school education. Many acquire their skills through apprenticeship training programs, through experience gained on the job, or by completing a vocational-school curriculum.

Earnings of skilled workers are relatively high, reflecting the level of work they are required to perform, their extensive training, and the exercise of independent judgment. They generally have more job security, better chances for promotions, and more opportunities to open their own businesses than do semiskilled or unskilled workers.

Employment growth in the period 1974–85 for the skilled group is expected to be 20 percent.

Semiskilled Occupations

Although employment growth in this group, which includes factory workers as well as operators of motor vehicles, will grow by only about 10 percent over the 1974–85 period, many thousands of job opportunities will be available to young people. This is the largest of all the occupational groups, and replacement needs are high.

Drivers and deliverers account for roughly one out of every five semiskilled workers. Employment of local and over-the-road truck-drivers is expected to grow, offering many employment opportunities for young men seeking to enter the work force.

A LOOK AT FUTURE MANPOWER SUPPLY

Just as the country's population furnishes the market for most of the goods and services it produces, it also provides the men and women who produce those goods and services.

The labor force, that part of our population aged 16 and over who are working or looking for work, is expected to reach a total of 108,000,000 by 1985, a growth of more than 18 percent over 1974.

The rising proportion of working women will continue to be a major factor (along with the growth in the number of young workers) contributing to the expected increase in the labor force. The highest proportion of working women is found in the 45-to-54 age group.

Changes in the Labor Force

Changes in the labor force during the next decade will greatly affect the teenagers of today. By 1985, more than one-fourth of all persons between 16 and 21 will be in the labor force. This would include those serving in the armed forces. In 1955, one-fifth of all persons in this age group were employed.

The key words will be *education* and *training*. Of the young people who will be working at the end of the next decade, more will have completed high school, college, and other higher learning than ever before. School dropouts are more likely to be unemployed than will be graduates.

Aside from the loss of earnings that the poorly educated worker experiences over his lifetime, he will not share in the other benefits that result from a good education: cultural enrichment, a satisfying way of life both as a worker and a responsible citizen, and other intangible social advantages.

Of course, all of the above projections are based upon a continu-

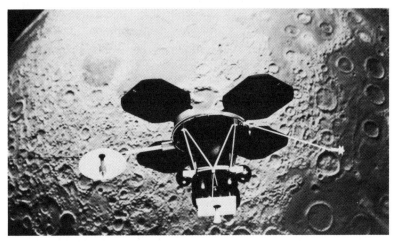

Space exploration will provide many jobs in the coming decade.

ance of the high economic level, advancement in technology, and continued employment. Nevertheless, proper preparation will make you ready for a labor market with a scarcity of jobs and a scarcity of skills. You must have a salable skill that will hold up in a tight labor market. The choice is yours.

What About the Girls?

The last decade has seen a great surge of job equality for women. This goes beyond the usual occupations we normally think of. Women made rapid advances in sports (jockeys and baseball umpires), as airline pilots, as executives in the business world, space travel (Soviet cosmonaut), and in high-ranking government and military positions.

It has traditionally been a man's world, and it is my opinion that employers are finally beginning to recognize the value of this untapped labor supply. The recognition came about by accident as well as by legislation. When confronted with labor shortages, employers hired women in traditionally men's jobs and were surprised (or were they?) to discover that women could hold their own.

A word of caution, girls. If you want equal rights and opportunities, you must be able to take the liabilities that go along with them. No special treatment. You're up to it, and the 1980's will prove this. Think big! Think beyond the usual female occupations.

If you perform jobs equal to male jobs, expect and ask for equal pay and benefits.

What Other Jobs of the Future?

You can expect the following areas to provide challenging jobs during the 1980's. Scientific advancement moves so rapidly that what formerly took twenty or twenty-five years to develop (pure research to finished product) now takes five years or less.

Ocean Studies. Not only will there be exploration of the seas, but the ocean floor will be used for aquaculture and the farming of fish and salt-water proteins.

Arctic Studies. The arctic regions will be studied and utilized for mineral and oil production.

Computer Technology. Computers will continue their meteoric rise in usage. Many new vistas will open for both industrial and home use.

Space Technology. Great achievements will be made in communications, weather reporting, and interplanetary study.

Nuclear Power. Nuclear power will be translated into many new uses for transportation, fuel, and power supplies.

Pollution Control. Perhaps pollution control will be developed as a defense mechanism. Nevertheless, scientific advancements and job opportunities will occur.

Electronics. This will take in the whole spectrum: computers, home appliances, communications, television, medical advances, laser techniques.

Medical Advances. There will be organ transplants, new methods of birth control, greater immunization, breakthroughs to incurable diseases. So much can happen!

Transportation. Local, national, even international transportation systems will make new advances. We will see electric-drive vehicles, nuclear power, high-speed railways.

Location of Increased Labor and Jobs

Basically, projected labor forces by states show that, during the next decade, those states with wide open spaces will have the greatest increases in labor. Since population growths go hand in hand with growth in labor force, study the following table to show where you might want to go to seek a job or pursue a career.

State	Projected % Increase in Population Growth
Nevada	39.6
Arizona	24.0
Florida	24.0
California	23.0
Maryland	21.0
New Hampshire	18.0
Colorado	18.0
Delaware	18.0
Connecticut	17.0
Alaska	17.0
South Dakota	0.0
North Dakota	0.0
West Virginia	0.0
Mississippi	1.0
Maine	2.0
Iowa	3.0
Pennsylvania	3.0
Wyoming	3.0
Montana	4.0
Kansas	4.0

So—take your choice! What do you want to do? Where do you want to go? You have the opportunity and the challenge. It is up to you to make the decision.